Drag and Drop
HTML

Davinder Singh Minhas

STERLING PUBLISHERS PVT. LTD.
A-59, Okhla Industrial Area, Phase-II, New Delhi
Ph.: 26386165, 26387070, 26386209
Fax: 91-11-26383788
E-mail: mail@sterlingpublishers.com
Website: www.sterlingpublishers.com

ISBN: 978-81-207-5735-6
© 2011, HTML
All rights reserved. No part of this publication may be reproduced, stored in a retrieval system, or transmitted, in any form or by any means, electronic, mechanical, photocopying, recording or otherwise, without the prior permission of the original publishers.

Printed at Sterling Publishers Private Limited., New Delhi-110020. India

Contents

Introduction	5
Formatting a web page	13
Adding images to a web page	28
Horizontal rule	37

1. Introduction

Short for **HyperText Markup Language**, **HTML** is a computer language widely used for creating web pages. Thus, a web page is also called an HTML document.

HTML is a system for making or tagging a document that indicates its logical structure and gives instructions for its layout on the page for electronic transmission and display. HTML documents have an **.html** or **.htm** extention. For example, **index.html**.

You can display HTML documents on any type of computer, such as a Macintosh or IBM-compatible computer. You do not have to create separate HTML documents for different types of computers. These documents transfer quickly over the web.

HTML TAGS

Angle brackets < > are used for enclosing each HTML tag and for giving it a specific instruction. Most tags have an opening tag and a closing tag that affect the text between the tags. The closing tag has a forward slash (/). However, some tags have only an opening tag. Uppercase or lowercase letters can also be used for typing tags.

> **<TITLE> Sterling Publications </TITLE>**

HTML ATTRIBUTES

Some tags have attributes that offer options for the tag. For example, the <FONT> tag has a COLOR attribute that allows you change the colour of your text.

> **<FONT COLOR="#0000FF">**

Drag and Drop Series

SOFTWARE FOR CREATING A WEB PAGE

There are several types of programs to choose from while creating a web page.

Text Editor

To create and edit documents that contain only text, a **text editor** can be used. Advanced editing and formatting features are not present in this simple program. **Notepad** for Windows and **Simple Text** for Macintosh are well-known text editors.

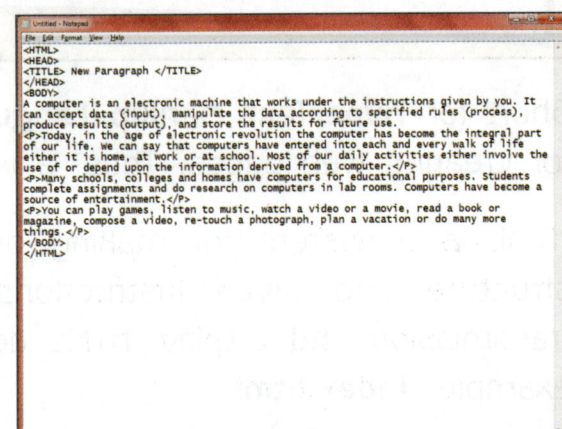

HTML Editor

HTML editors, such as **Microsoft FrontPage**, is a dedicated program for writing HTML code and managing web pages. These programs save your time for writing HTML code and offers a graphical environment for building web pages as well as a text-based environment. Most HTML editors will also colour your HTML tags for easy viewing of your code.

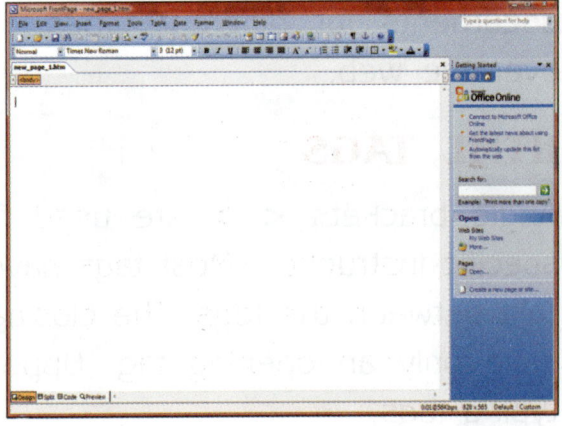

Word Processors

Advanced editing and formatting features are provided by a word processor. Any formatting you apply to the text will not appear when you view your documents on the web, unless the formatting is given in the form of a tag. **Microsoft Word** and **Corel WordPerfect** are some of the word processors. When using a text editor or word processor, you must first type the text for the web page and then add HTML tags to specify how you want the text to appear on the web page.

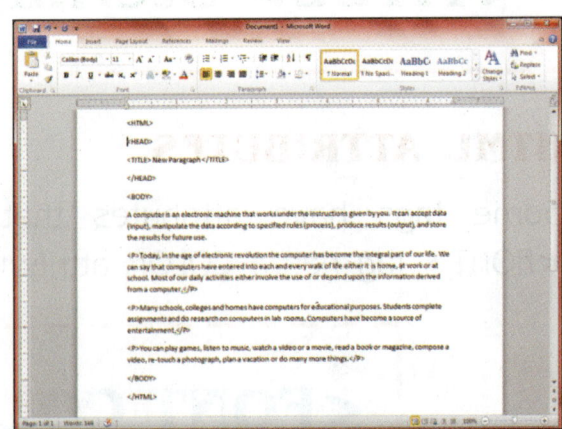

6

HTML

CREATING AND SAVING A WEB PAGE

Open the text editor or word processor that you will use to create a web page. In the following example, we will work in Microsoft WordPad.

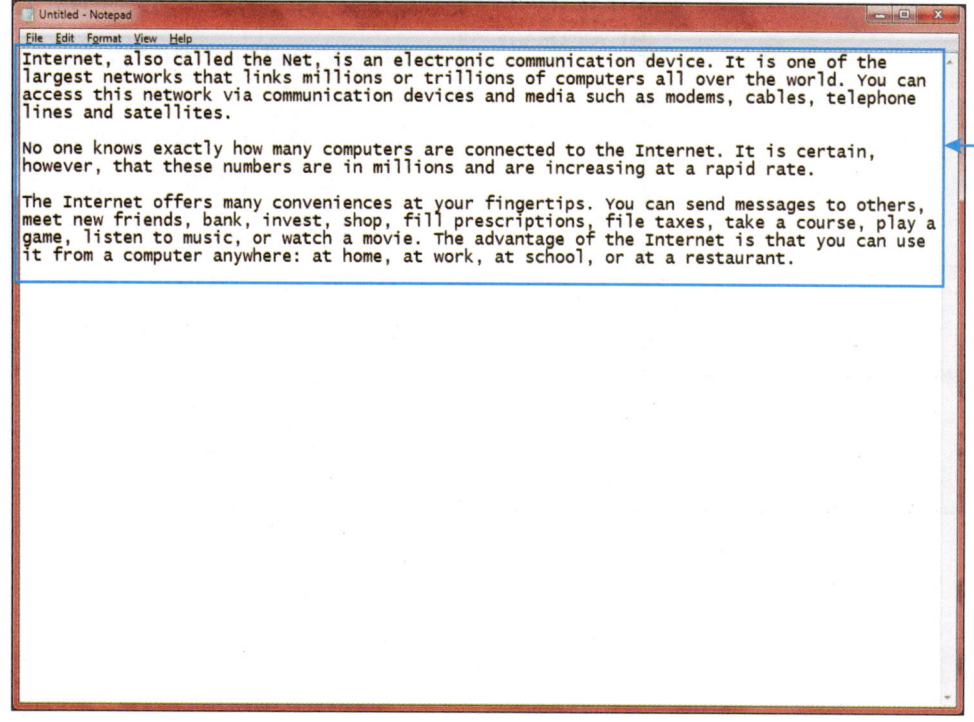

1. Type the text that you want to display on the web page.

   In order to format the text, you must use HTML tags.

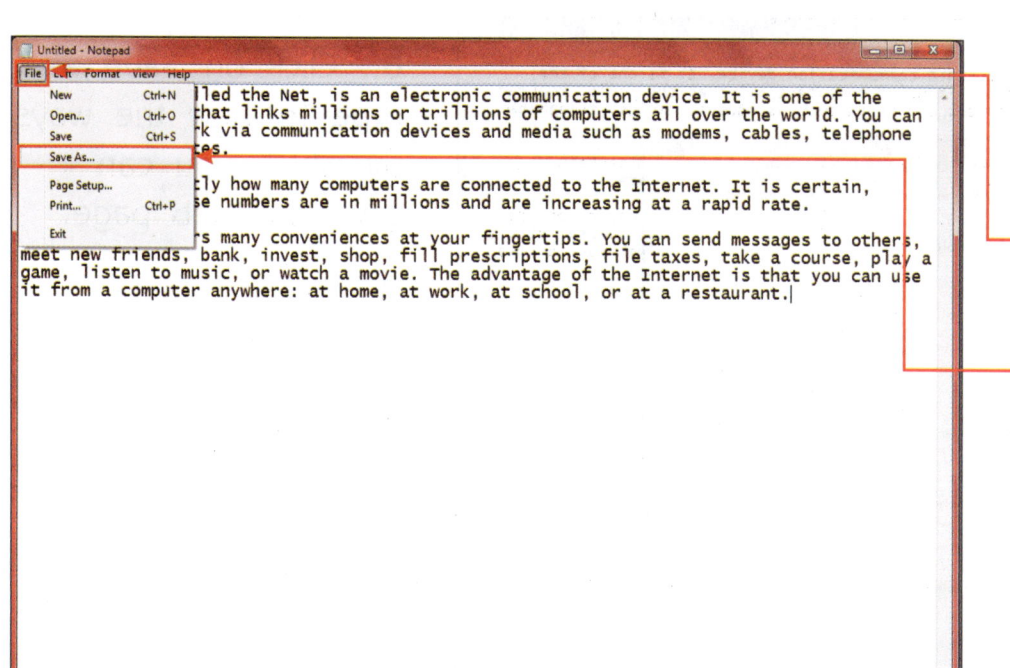

2. Check the web page for any spelling and grammar errors.

3. Click on **File** in the menu bar.

4. Click on **Save As** to save the web page.

   *The **Save As** dialog box appears.*

7

Drag and Drop Series

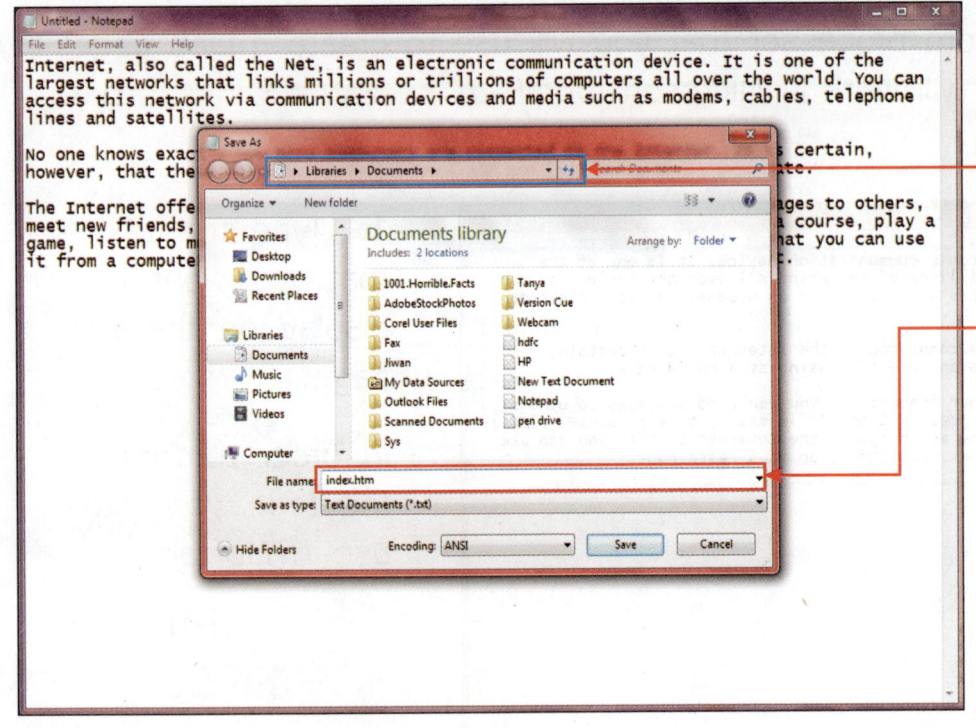

This area shows the location where the program will store the web page. You can click on this area to change the location.

5. Type a name for the web page. Make sure you add the **.html** or **.htm** extension to the web page-name.

A web page-name contains letters and numbers, but no spaces.

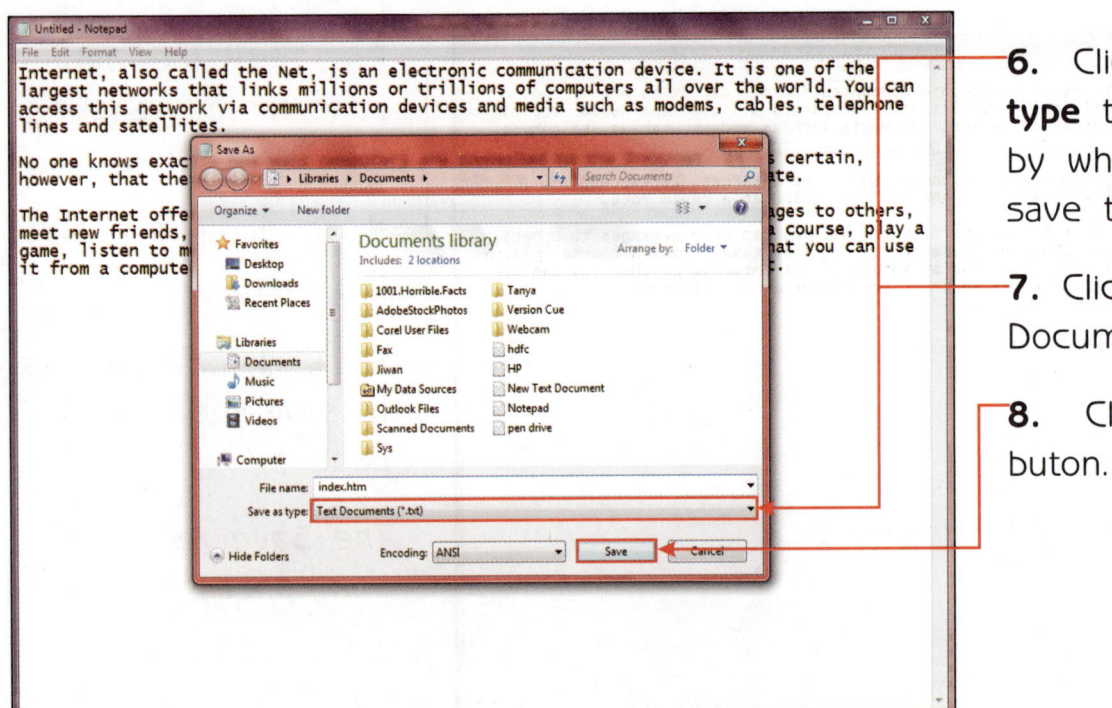

6. Click on **Save as type** to view the ways by which you can save the web page.

7. Click on Text Document.

8. Click on the **Save** buton.

BASIC TAGS

HTML Tags

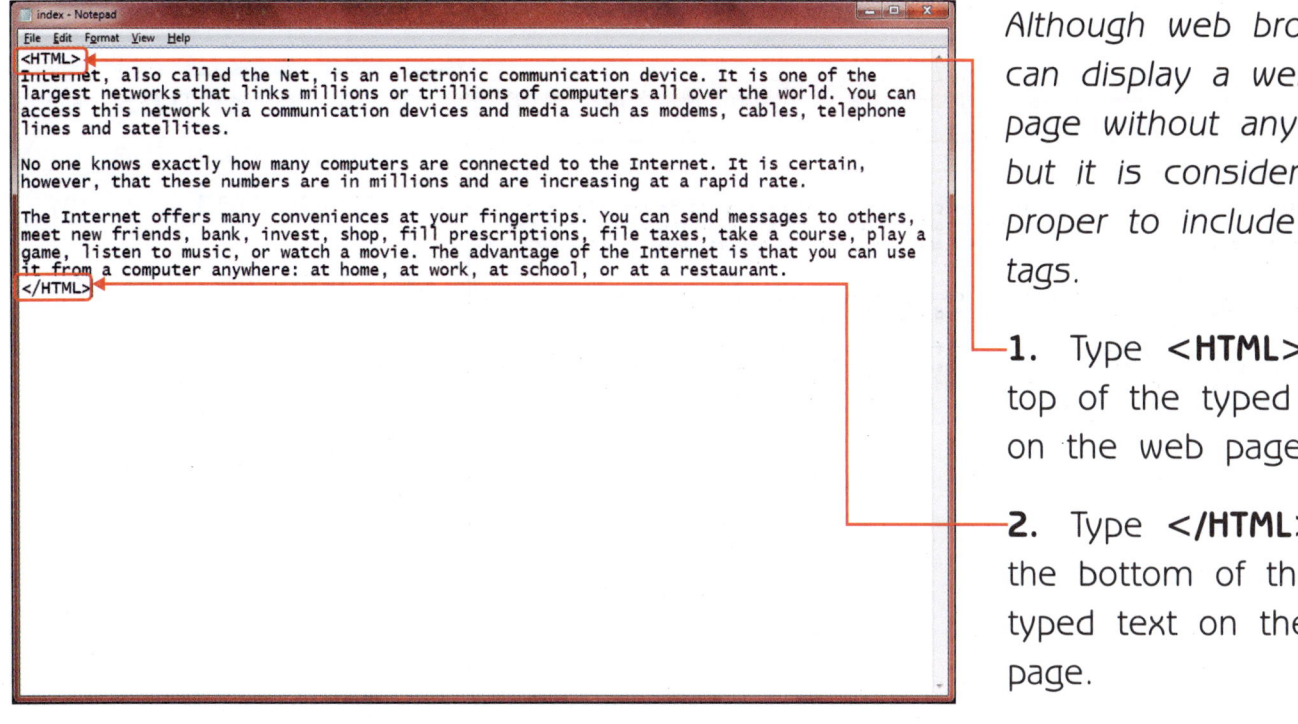

Although web browsers can display a web page without any tag, but it is considered proper to include these tags.

1. Type **<HTML>** on top of the typed text on the web page.

2. Type **</HTML>** at the bottom of the typed text on the web page.

HEAD Tags

Any information about a web page, such as the title, is contained in the HEAD tag.

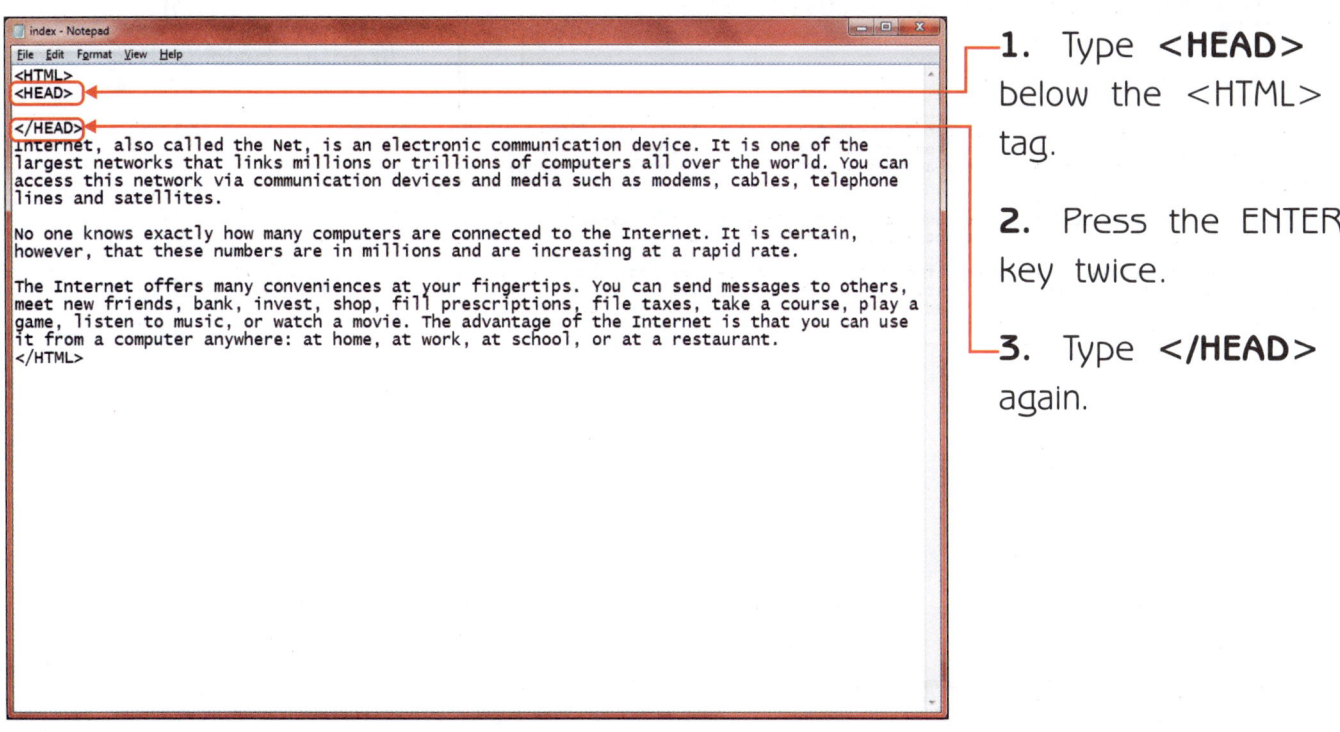

1. Type **<HEAD>** below the <HTML> tag.

2. Press the ENTER key twice.

3. Type **</HEAD>** again.

Drag and Drop Series

Title Tags

The contents of a web page is described by the **Title**. The title bar of a web browser window usually displays the title.

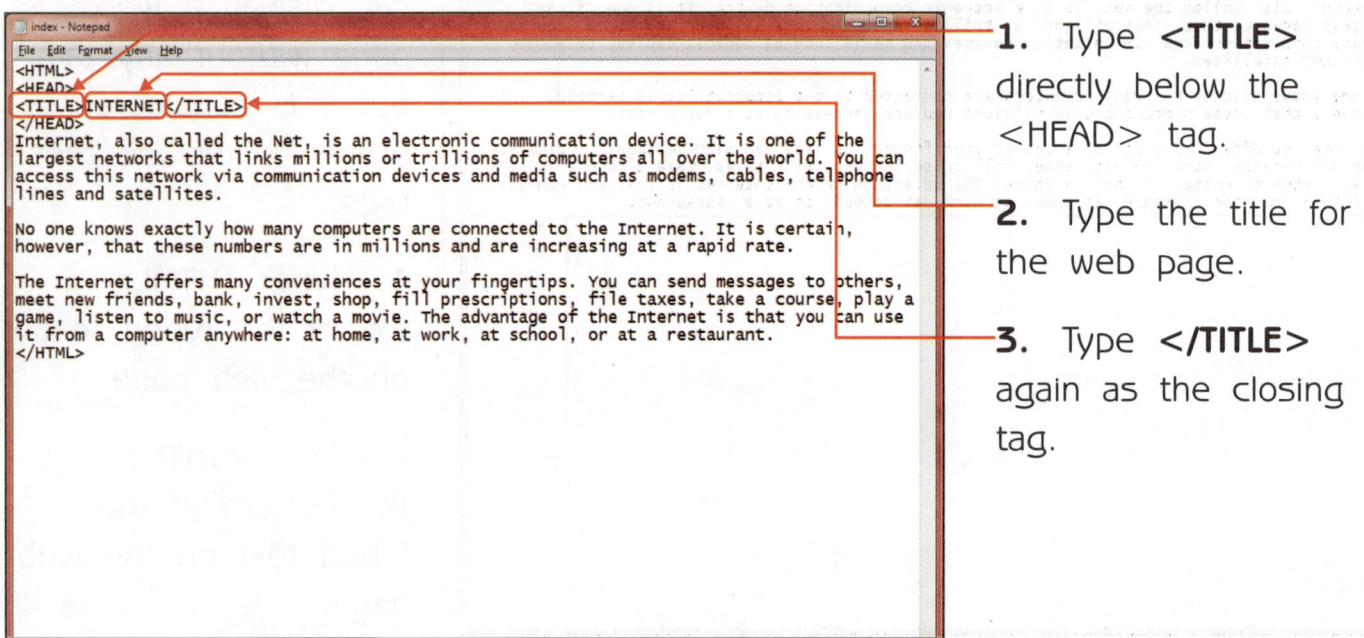

1. Type **<TITLE>** directly below the <HEAD> tag.

2. Type the title for the web page.

3. Type **</TITLE>** again as the closing tag.

Body Tags

After entering the Title tag, the next step is to enter the **Body** tag.

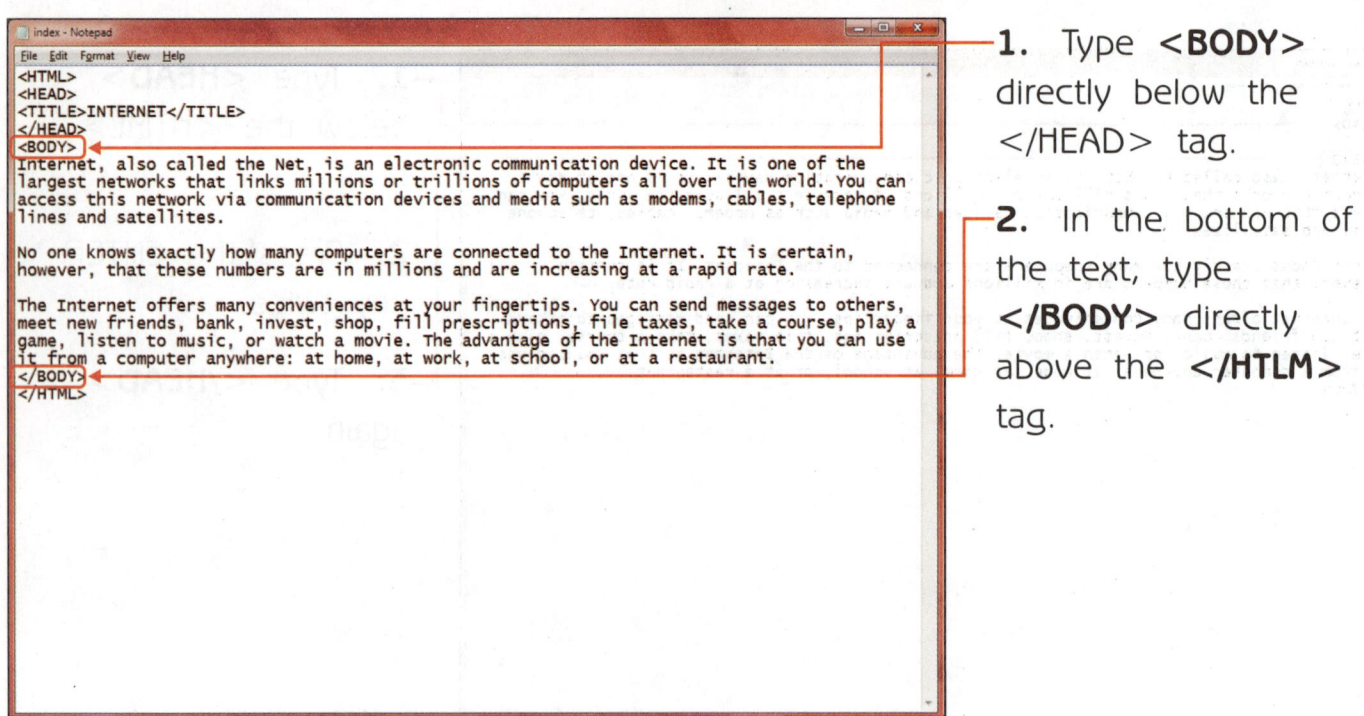

1. Type **<BODY>** directly below the </HEAD> tag.

2. In the bottom of the text, type **</BODY>** directly above the **</HTLM>** tag.

HTML

DISPLAYING A WEB PAGE IN A WEB BROWSER

You can also display a web page in a web browser. This will allow you to see how your web page will appear on the web.

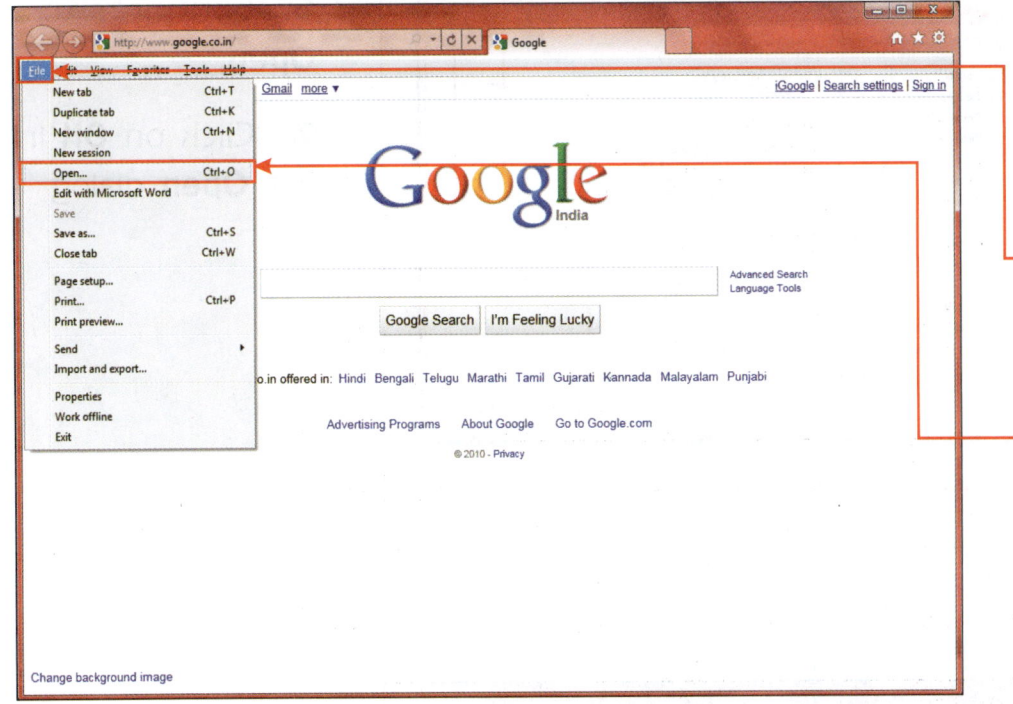

1. Press the **Alt** key on the keyboard to bring the Menu bar into the web browser.

2. Click on **File** to open your web page in the web Browser, .

3. Click on **Open**.

   *The **Open** dialog box will appear.*

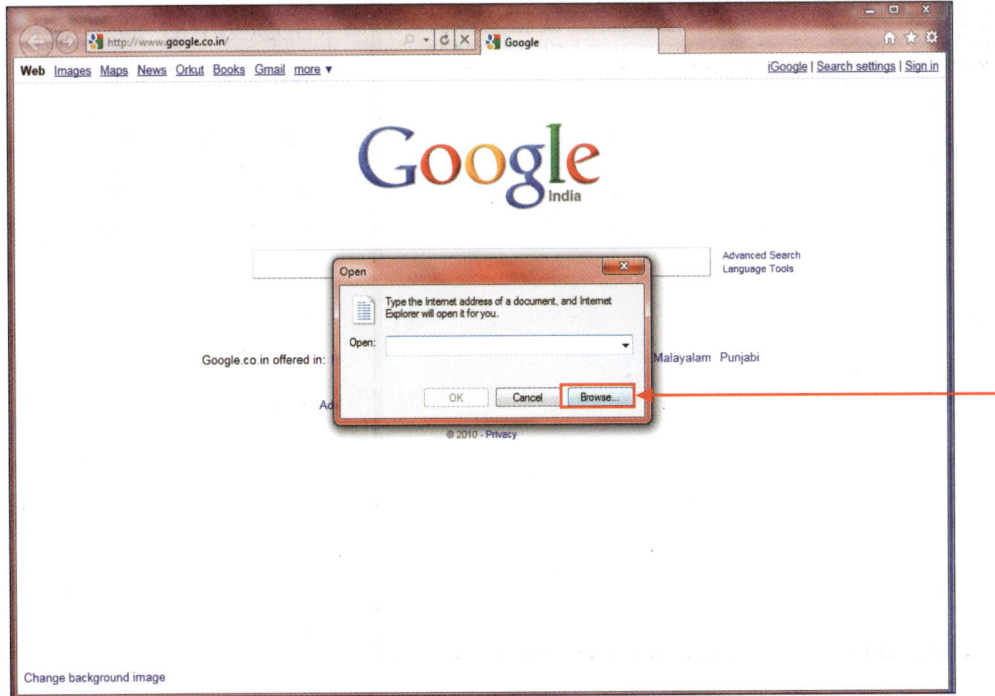

4. Click on **Browse** in the Open dialog box to locate the web page on your computer.

   *The **Microsoft Internet Explorer** dialog box appears.*

Drag and Drop Series

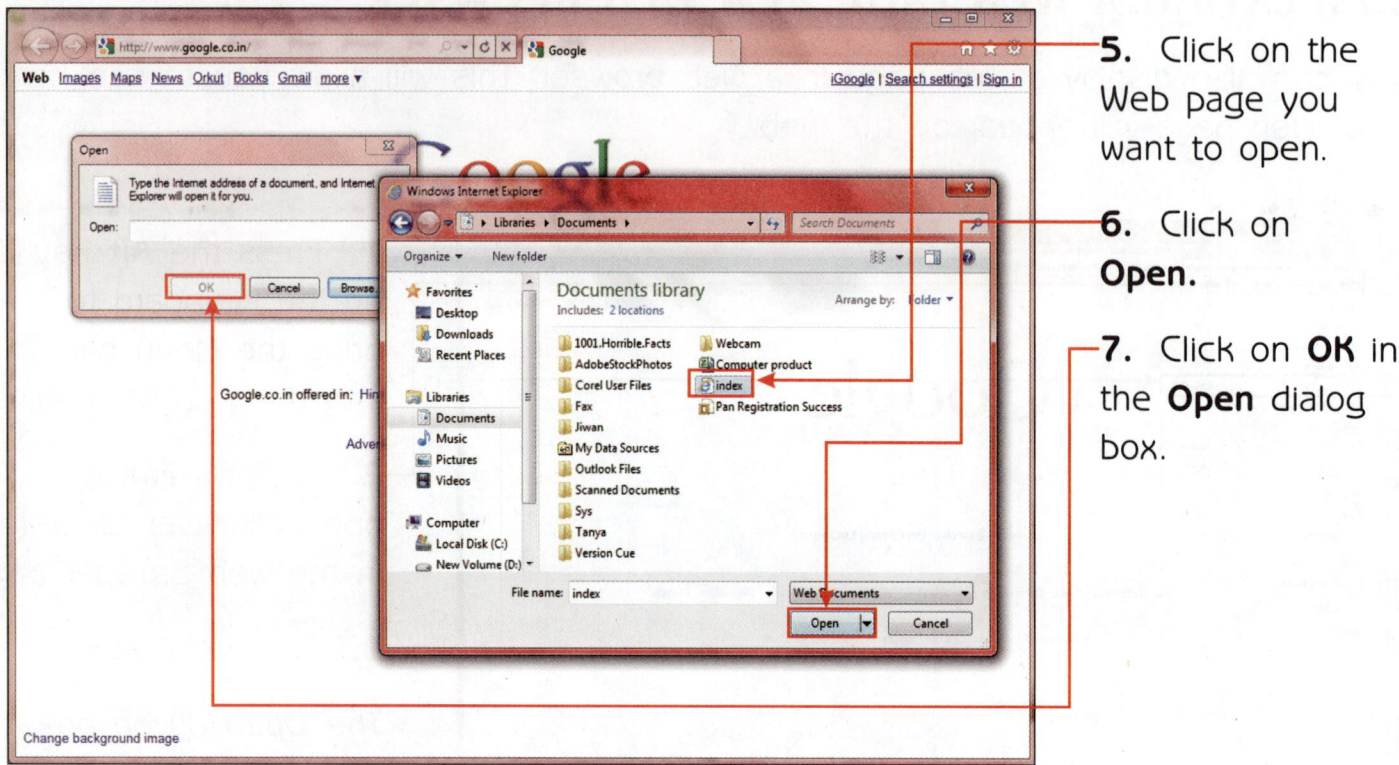

5. Click on the Web page you want to open.

6. Click on **Open.**

7. Click on **OK** in the **Open** dialog box.

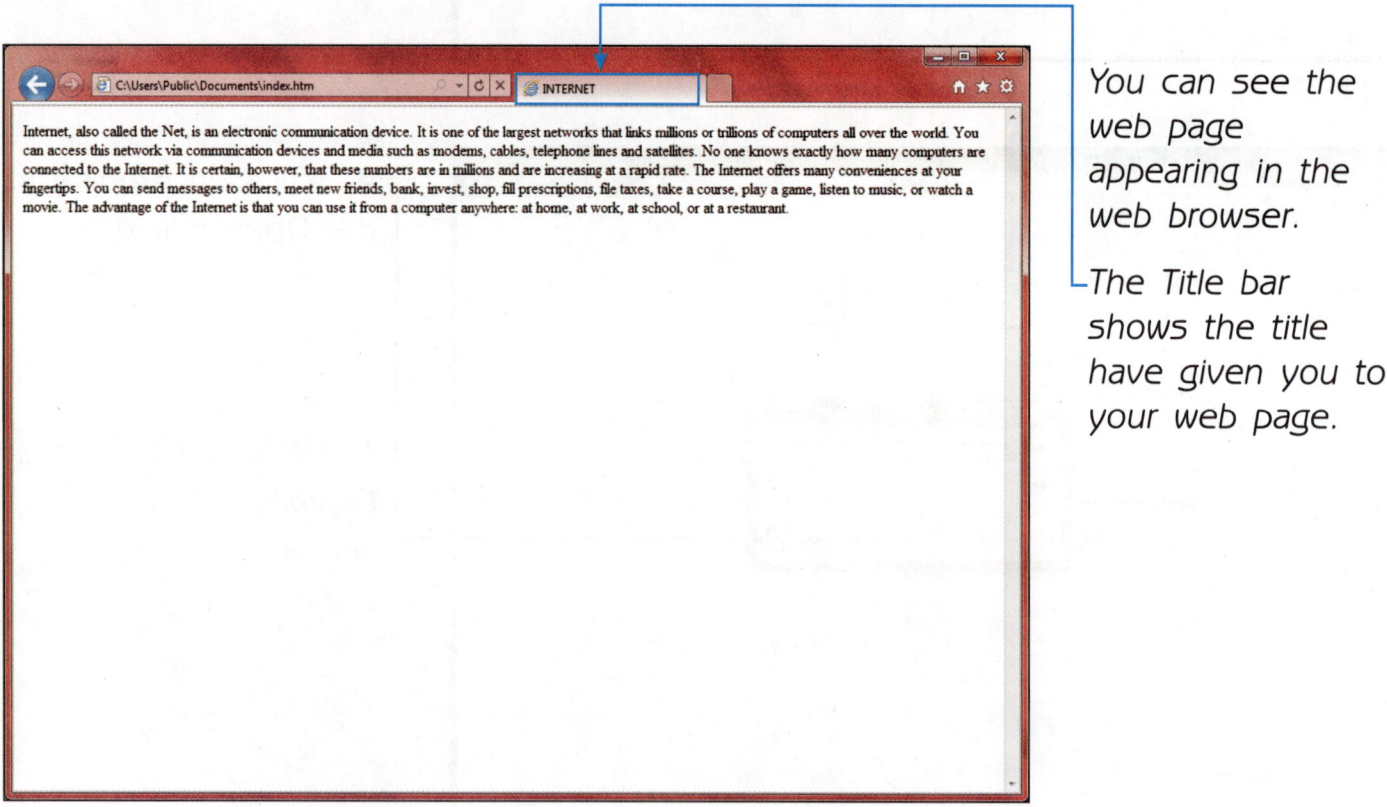

You can see the web page appearing in the web browser.

The Title bar shows the title have given you to your web page.

2 Formatting a web page

NEW PARAGRAPH

You must specify where to start a new paragraph while creating a web page.

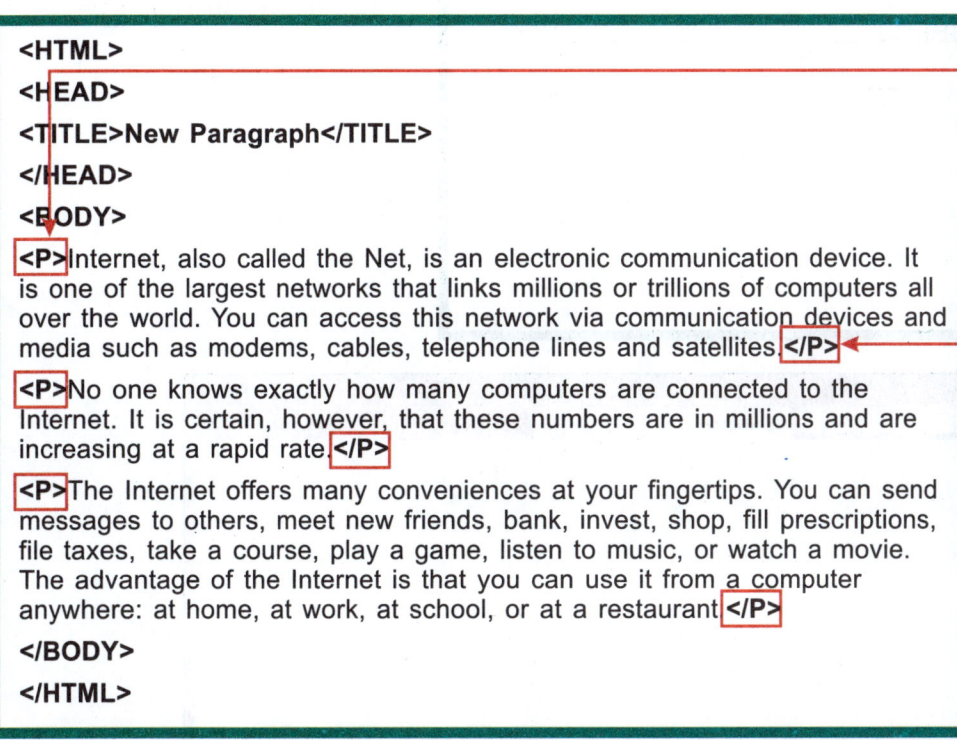

1. Type **<P>** before you begin each paragraph on your web page.

2. Type **</P>** at the end of each paragraph on your web page.

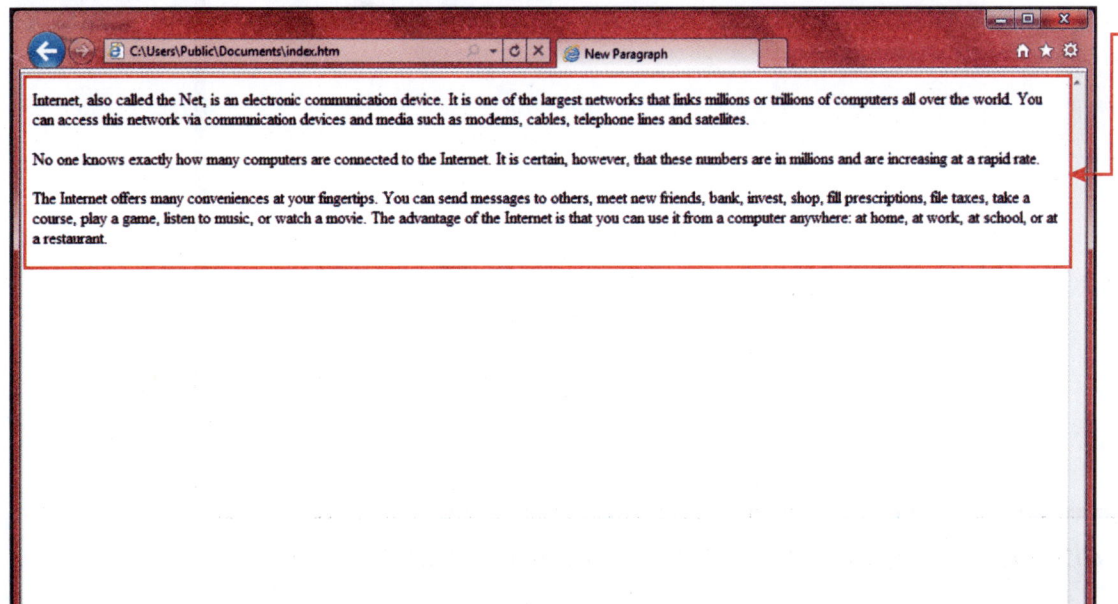

The web browser displays a blank line between each paragraph.

Drag and Drop Series

NEW LINE

While creating a web page, you must specify where to start each new line of the text.

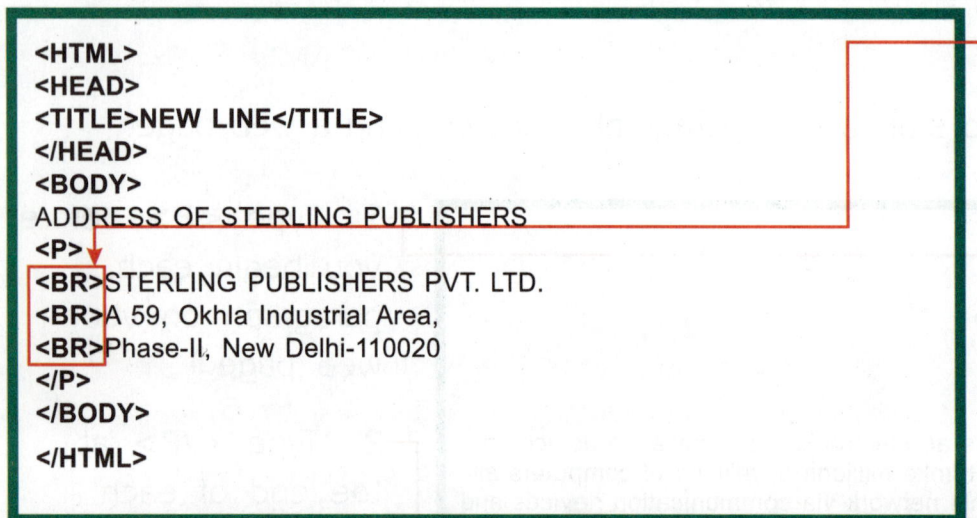

1. Type **
** before each line, which you want on a different line on your web page.

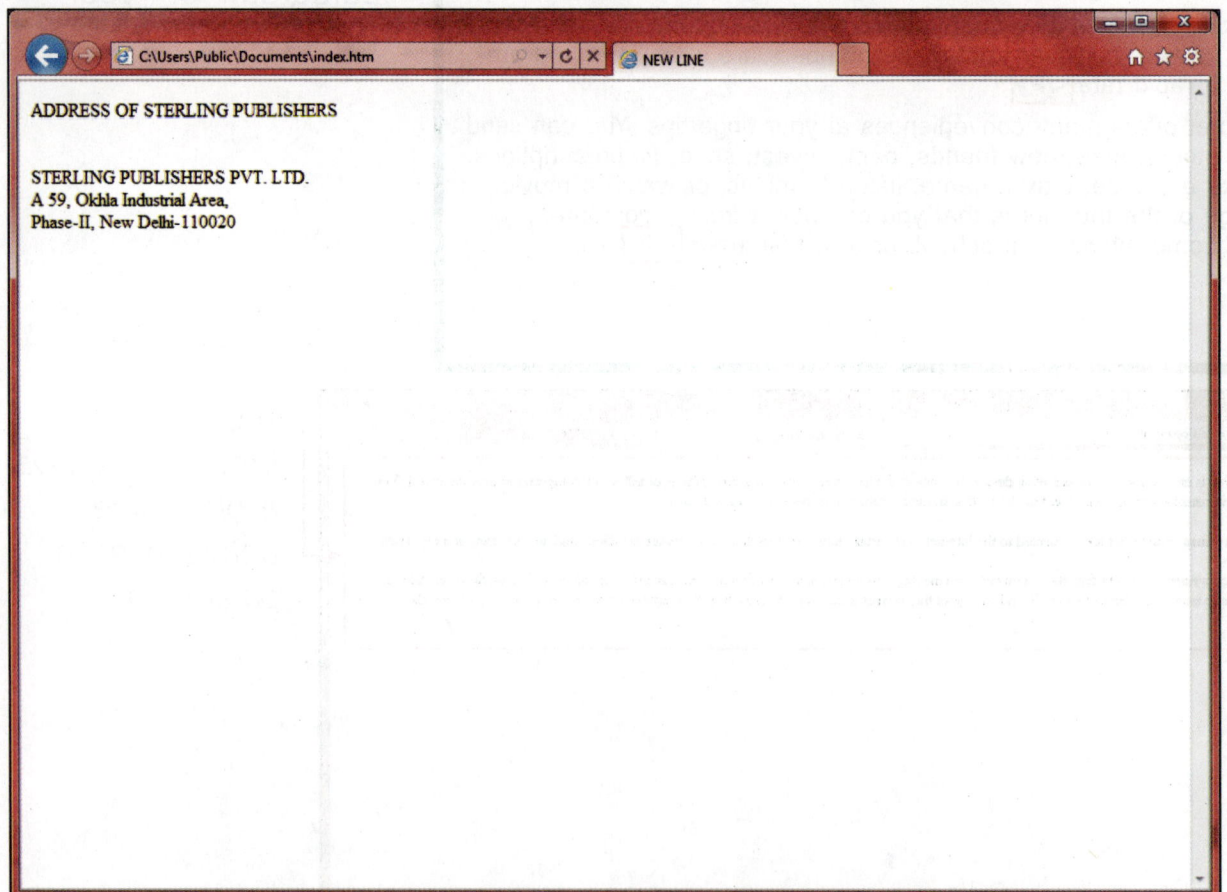

The web browser displays each line of the text on a new line.

HTML

ADDING A HEADING

You can add headings to display important information on the web. There are six different heading-levels to choose from.

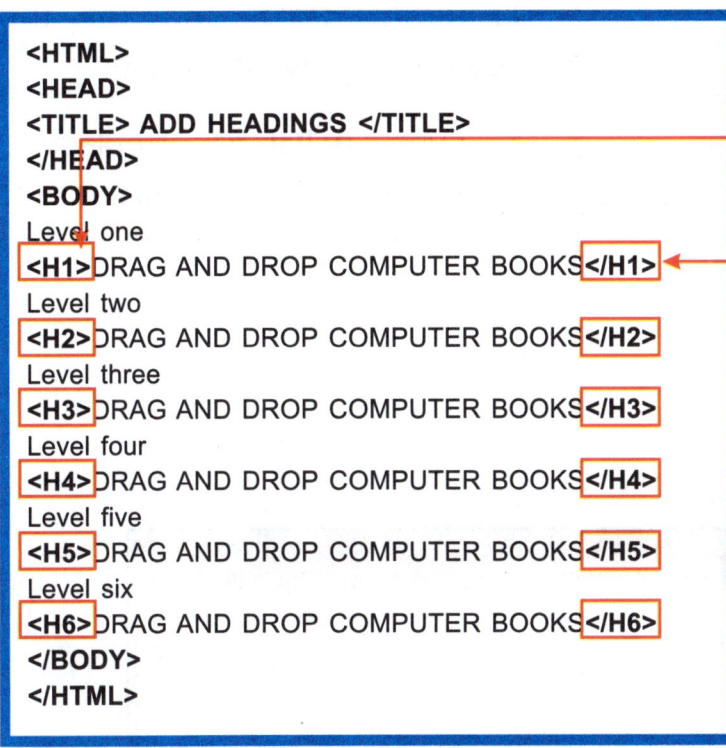

1. Type **<H*>** before the text you want to make a heading. Replace ***** with the heading-level numbered from 1 to 6.

2. Type **</H*>** after the text you want to make a heading. Replace ***** with the heading-level numbered from 1 to 6.

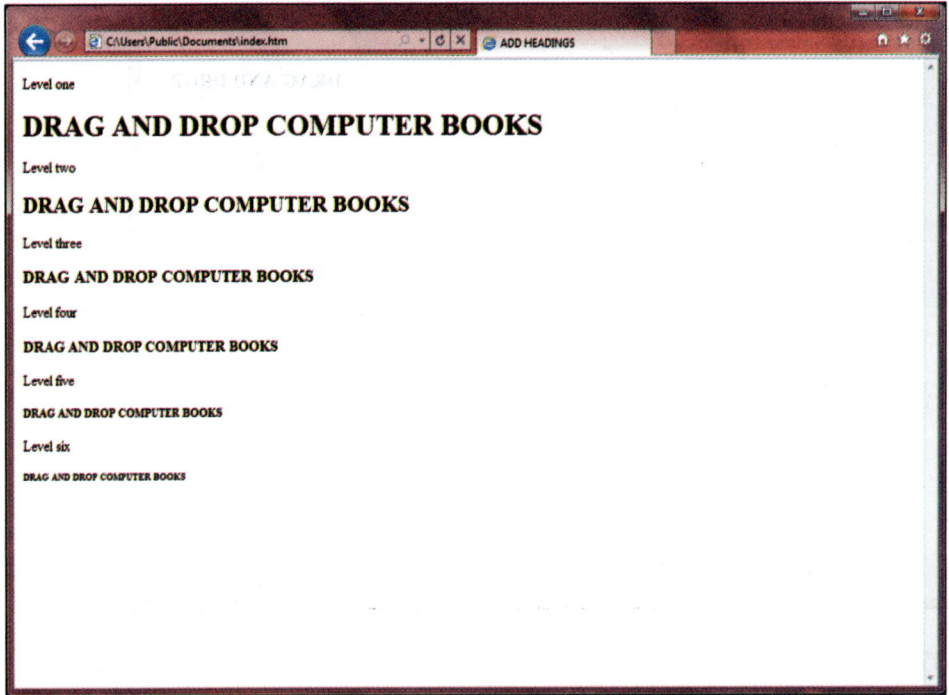

The web browser displays each line of the text with a different style of heading.

Drag and Drop Series

CHANGING THE ALIGNMENT OF THE HEADING

You can make the heading right, left or center aligned according to the demand of the web page.

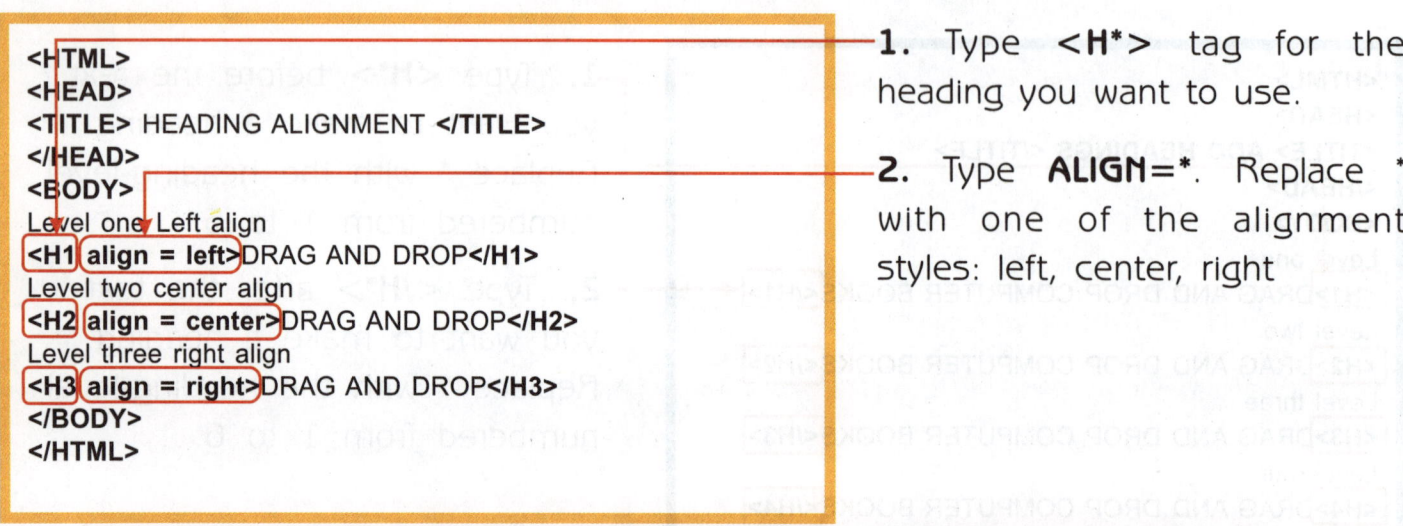

1. Type **<H*>** tag for the heading you want to use.

2. Type **ALIGN=***. Replace * with one of the alignment styles: left, center, right

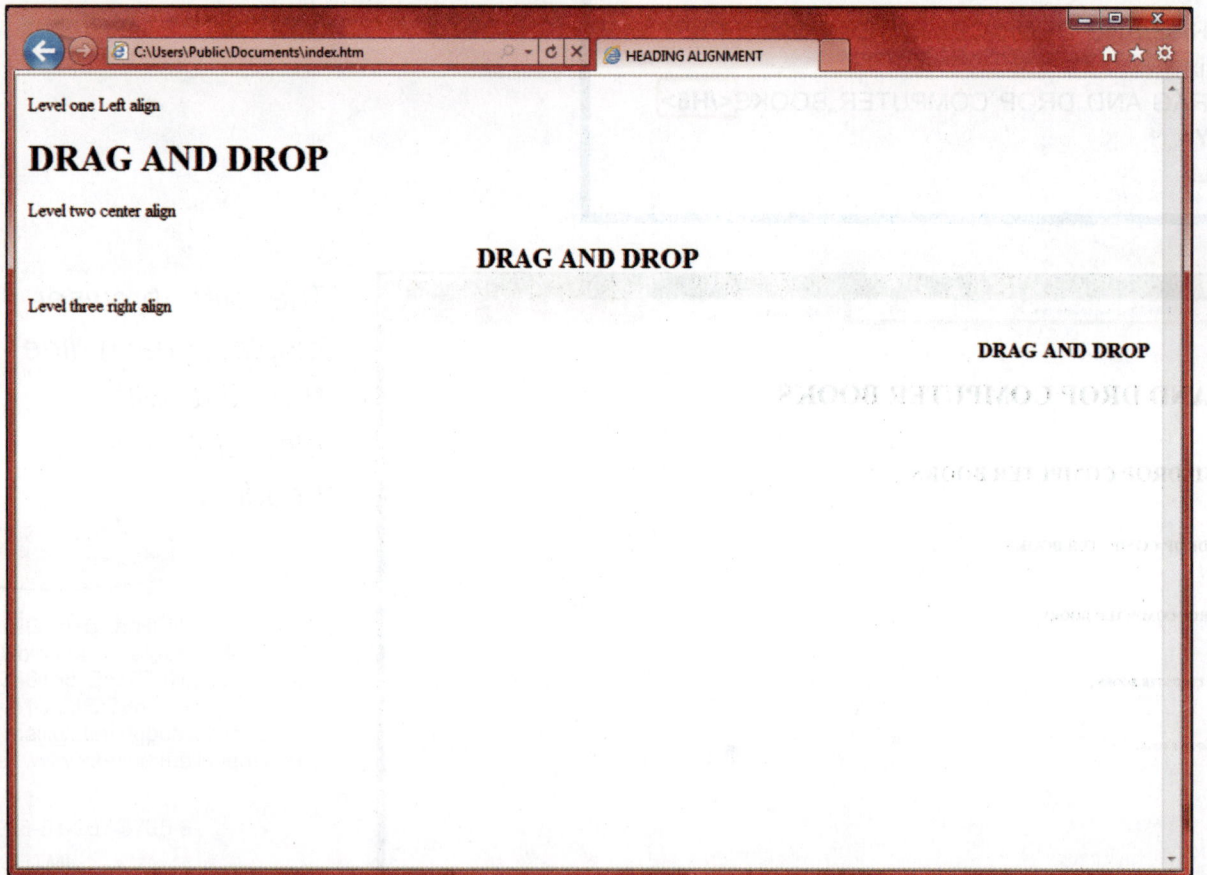

The heading, with the alignment you selected, is displayed by the web browser.

CENTER ALIGNING THE TEXT

By center aligning the text, we can emphasize on some important information.

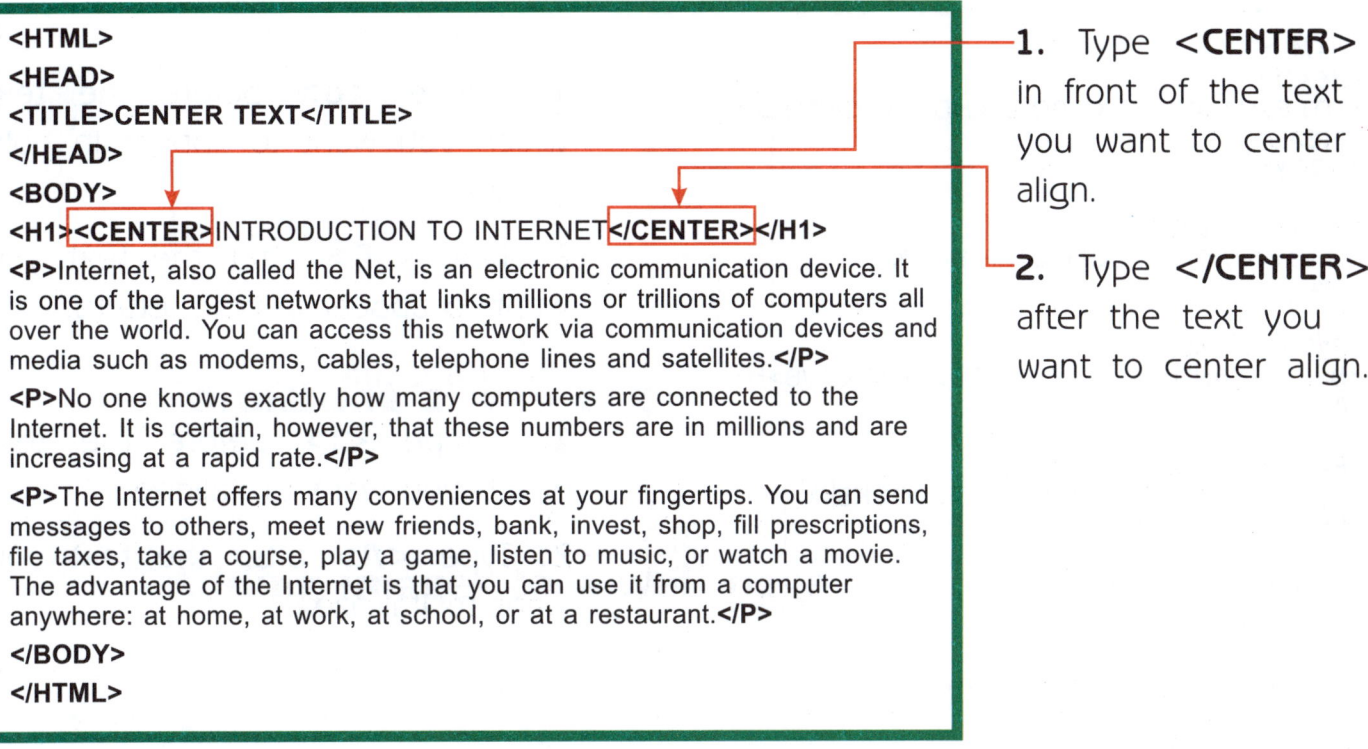

1. Type **<CENTER>** in front of the text you want to center align.

2. Type **</CENTER>** after the text you want to center align.

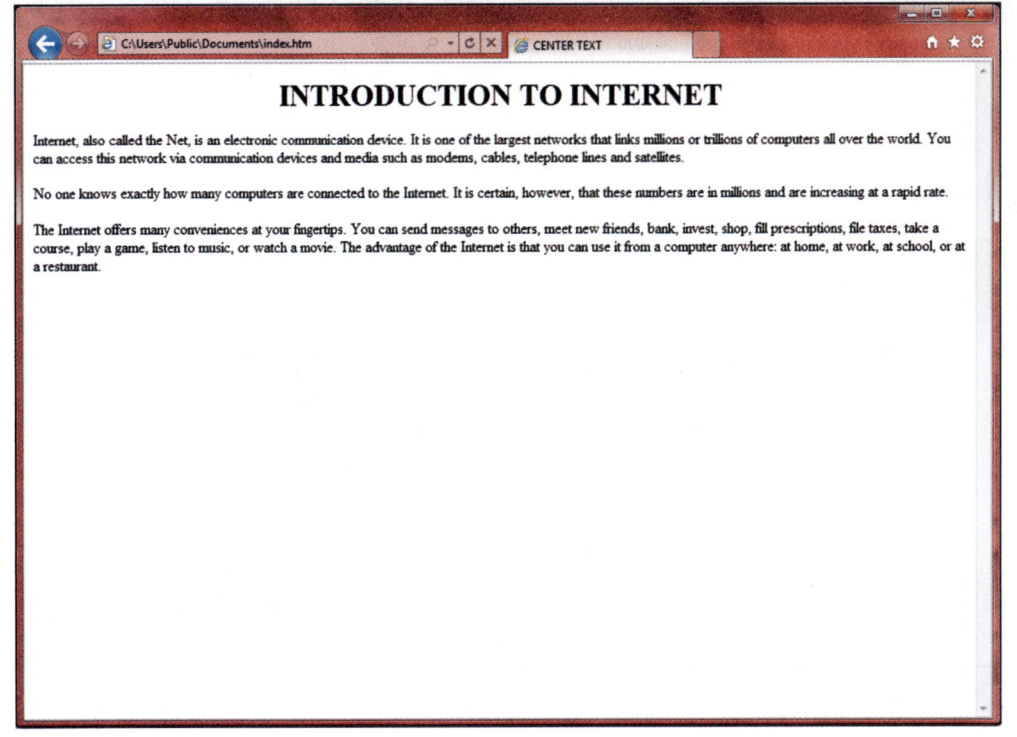

The text gets center aligned on the web page in your web browser.

Drag and Drop Series

MAKING BOLD OR ITALICIZING THE TEXT

You can change the appearance of the text by making it bold or italic to emphasize an important information on your web page.

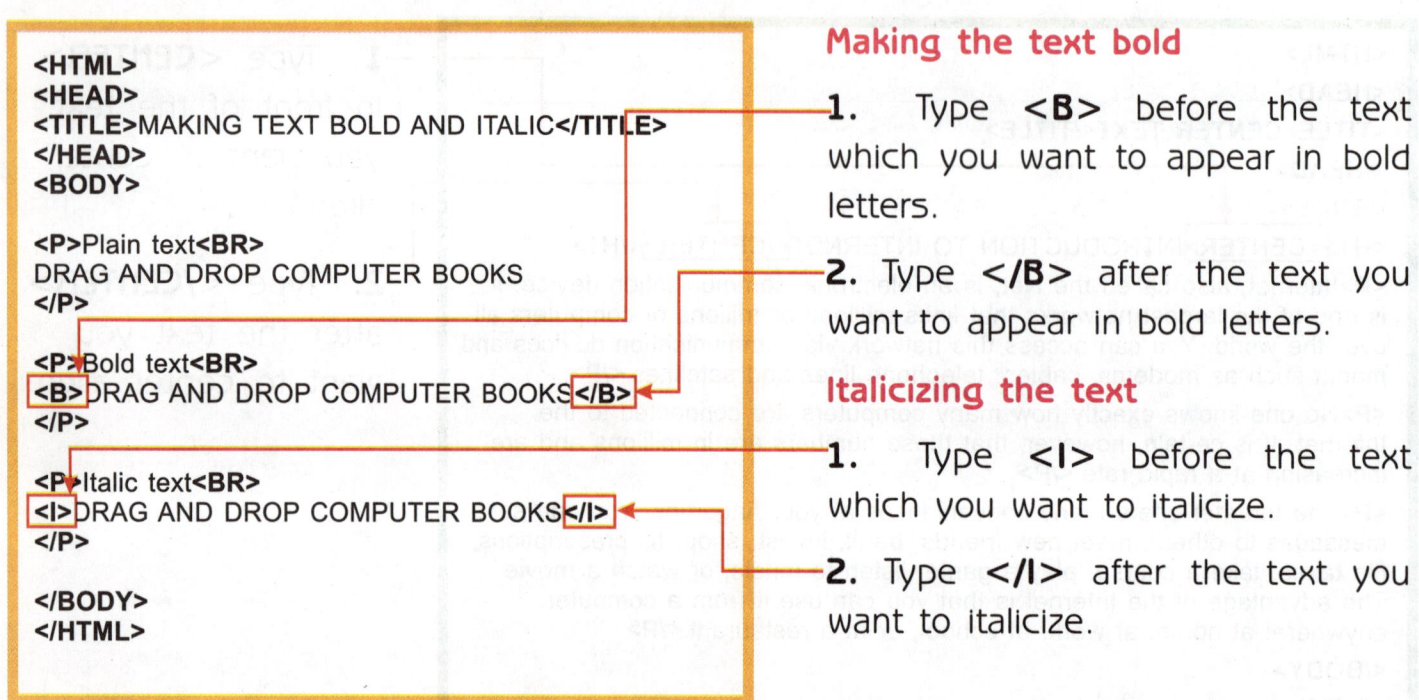

Making the text bold

1. Type **<B>** before the text which you want to appear in bold letters.

2. Type **</B>** after the text you want to appear in bold letters.

Italicizing the text

1. Type **<I>** before the text which you want to italicize.

2. Type **</I>** after the text you want to italicize.

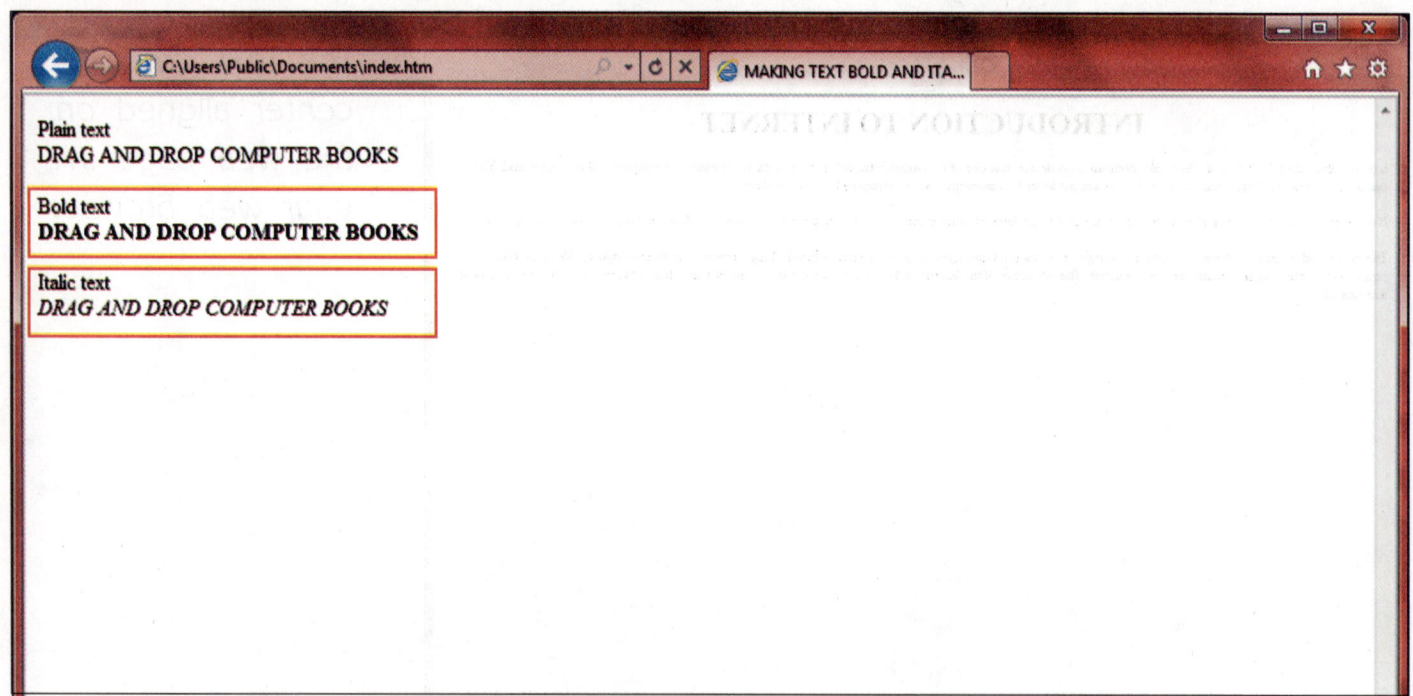

The bold or italic text is displayed by the web browser.

UNDERLINING OR STRIKING OUT THE TEXT

You can underline highlight some important information or you can even strike out parts in your text to make changes in the text to highlight it .

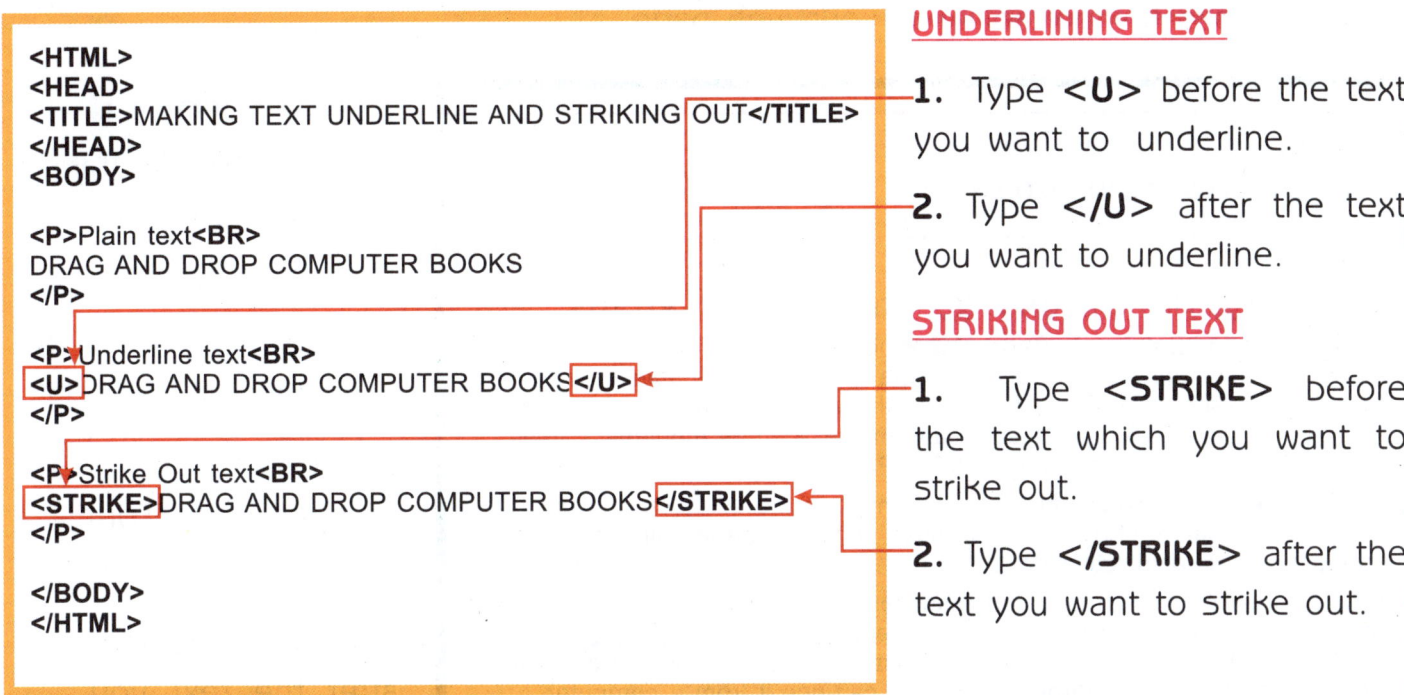

UNDERLINING TEXT

1. Type **<U>** before the text you want to underline.

2. Type **</U>** after the text you want to underline.

STRIKING OUT TEXT

1. Type **<STRIKE>** before the text which you want to strike out.

2. Type **</STRIKE>** after the text you want to strike out.

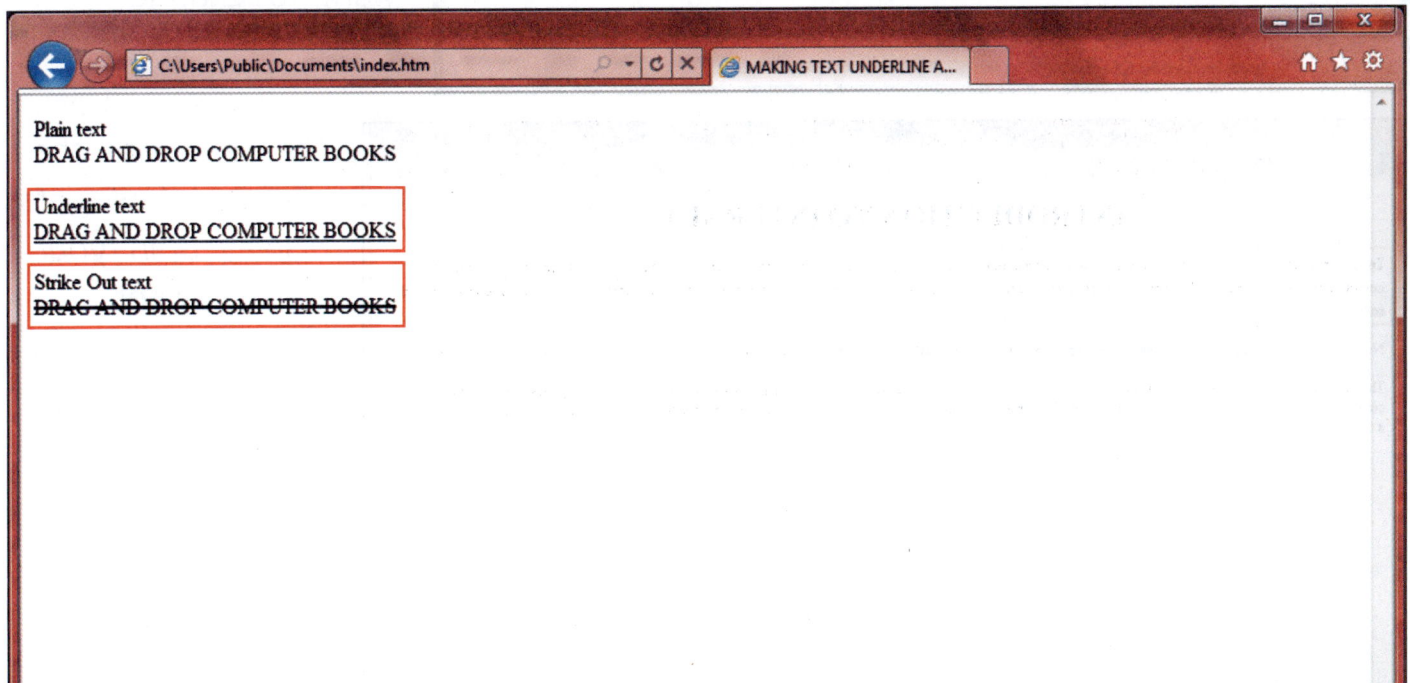

The underlined text or the text you have striked out is displayed by the web browser.

Drag and Drop Series

CHANGING THE FONT OF THE TEXT

You can change the font of your text in order to enhance its appearance. You should choose from common font styles such as Arial, Times New Roman, etc. This increases the portability of your web page.

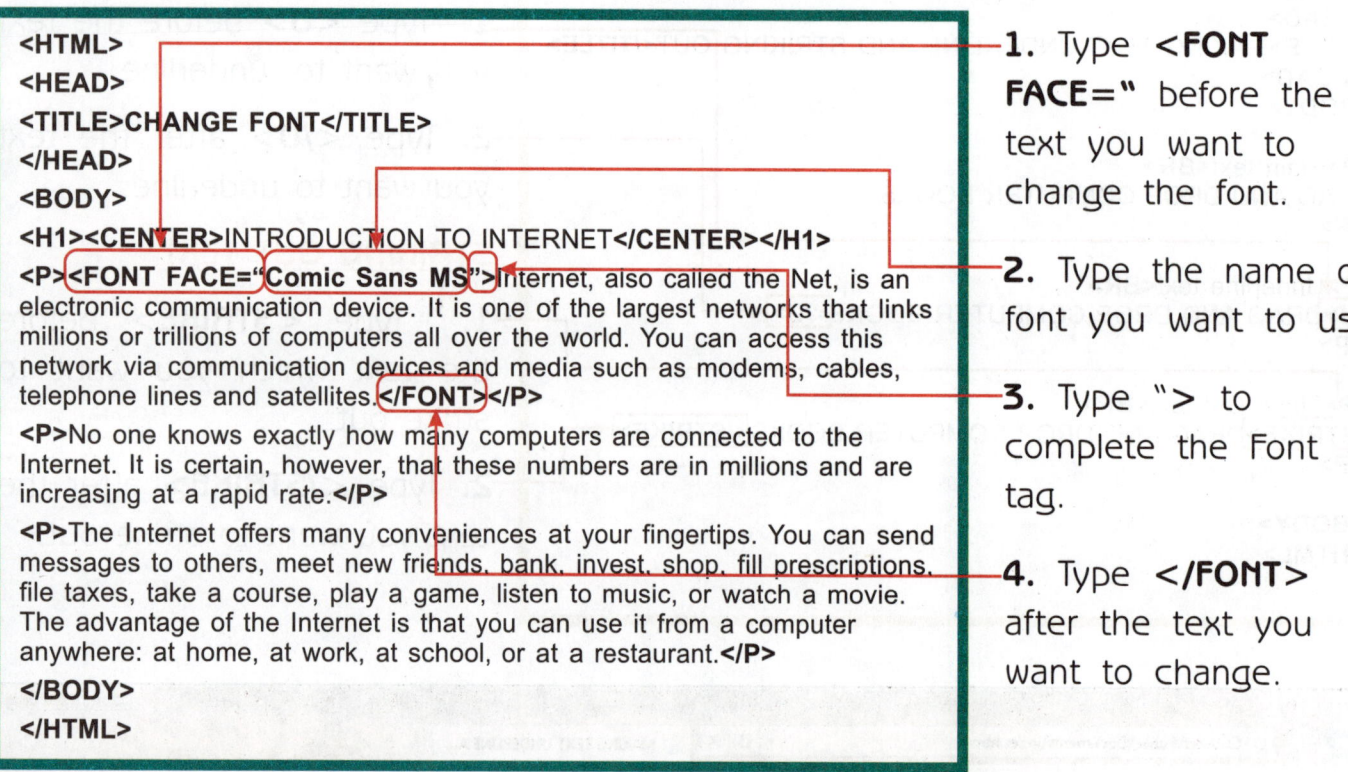

1. Type **<FONT FACE="** before the text you want to change the font.

2. Type the name of font you want to use.

3. Type **">** to complete the Font tag.

4. Type **</FONT>** after the text you want to change.

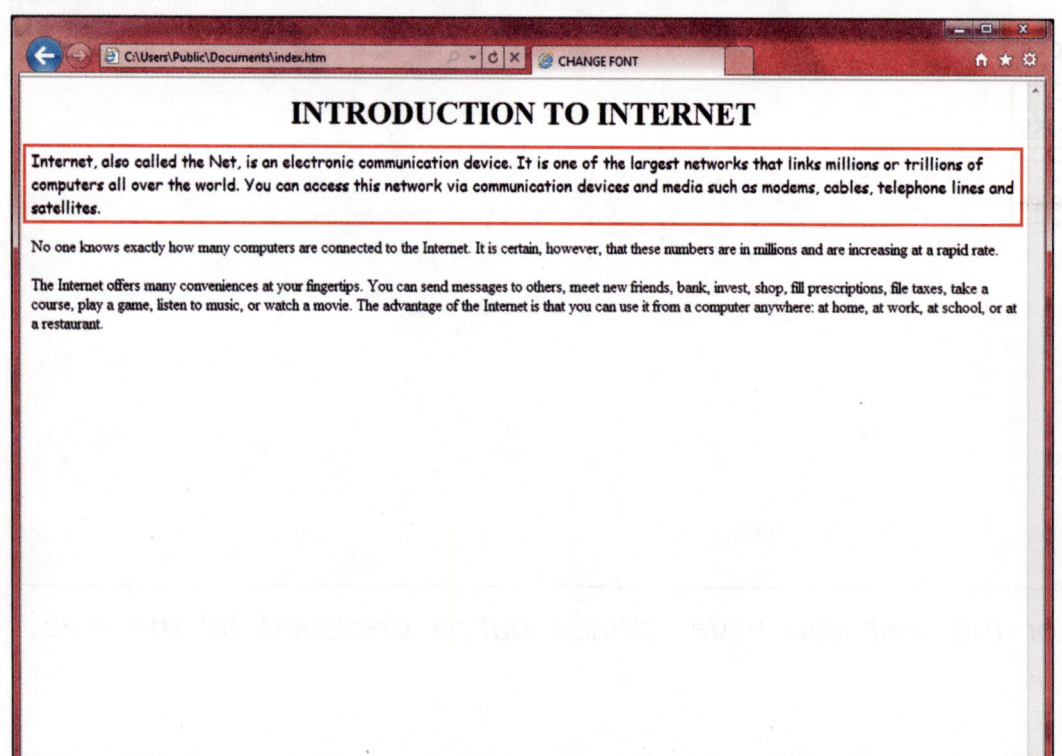

The text with the changed font gets displayed in your web browser.

CHANGING THE FONT SIZE

You can even change the size of text on your web page, just as you can change the font of the text. You can even change the size of individual characters on your web page.

```
<HTML>
<HEAD>
<TITLE> FONT SIZES </TITLE>
</HEAD>
<BODY>
<p>Font size one<BR>
<FONT SIZE="1">DRAG AND DROP</FONT>
</P>
<p>Font size two<BR>
<FONT SIZE="2">DRAG AND DROP</FONT>
</P>
<p>Font size three<BR>
<FONT SIZE="3">DRAG AND DROP</FONT>
</P>
<p>Font size four<BR>
<FONT SIZE="4">DRAG AND DROP</FONT>
</P>
<p>Font size five<BR>
<FONT SIZE="5">DRAG AND DROP</FONT>
</P>
<p>Font size six<BR>
<FONT SIZE="6">DRAG AND DROP</FONT>
</P>
<p>Font size seven<BR>
<FONT SIZE="7">DRAG AND DROP</FONT>
</P>
</BODY>
</HTML>
```

1. Type **<FONT SIZE="*">** before the text you want to change. Replace * with a number from 1 to 7. The smallest font size is 1 and the largest is 7.

2. Type **</FONT>** after the text you want to change.

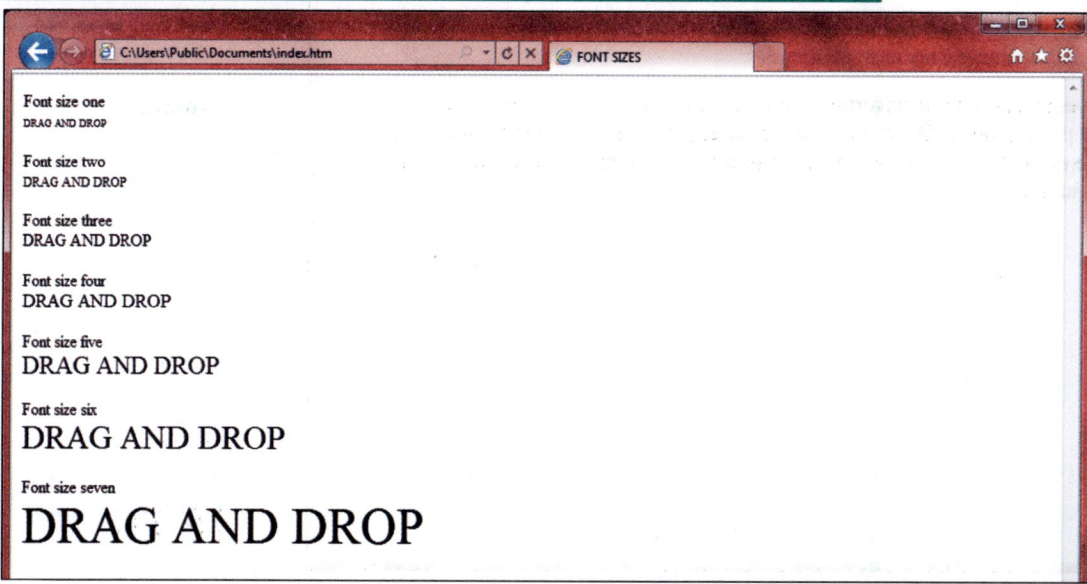

The Web browser displays the selected text in the new size.

Drag and Drop Series

CHANGING THE FONT SIZE OF THE WHOLE TEXT

The size of the whole text on your web page can also be changed.

```
<HTML>
<HEAD>
<TITLE>CHANGE FONT</TITLE>
</HEAD>
<BODY>
<BASEFONT SIZE="5">
<H1><CENTER>INTRODUCTION TO INTERNET</CENTER></H1>
<P>Internet, also called the Net, is an electronic communication device. It is one of the largest networks that links millions or trillions of computers all over the world. You can access this network via communication devices and media such as modems, cables, telephone lines and satellites.</P>
<P>No one knows exactly how many computers are connected to the Internet. It is certain, however, that these numbers are in millions and are increasing at a rapid rate.</P>
<P>The Internet offers many conveniences at your fingertips. You can send messages to others, meet new friends, bank, invest, shop, fill prescriptions, file taxes, take a course, play a game, listen to music, or watch a movie. The advantage of the Internet is that you can use it from a computer anywhere: at home, at work, at school, or at a restaurant.</P>
</BODY>
</HTML>
```

1. Type the <BASEFONT SIZE="?"> before the text on your web page. Replace **?** with a number from 1 to 7. The smallest size is 1 and the largest is 7.

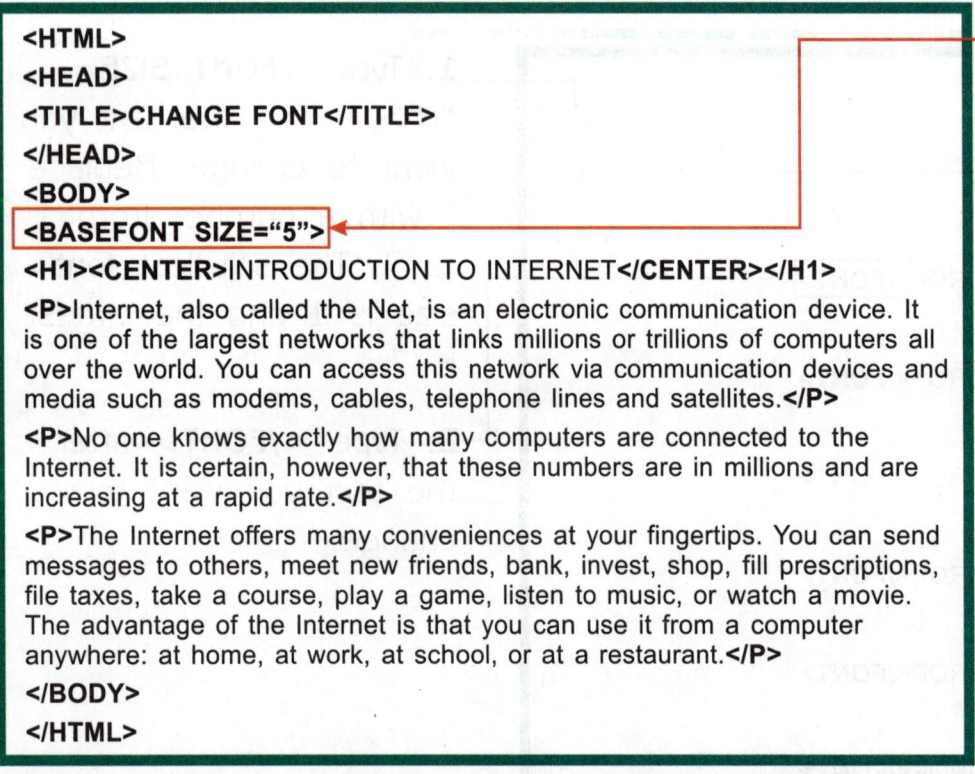

The web browser displays the text in the new size.

The BASEFONT tag does not affect the size of headings on your web page.

HTML

CHANGING THE COLOR OF TEXT

You can change the color of the whole text of your web page. You can create interesting text by changing the color of the text.

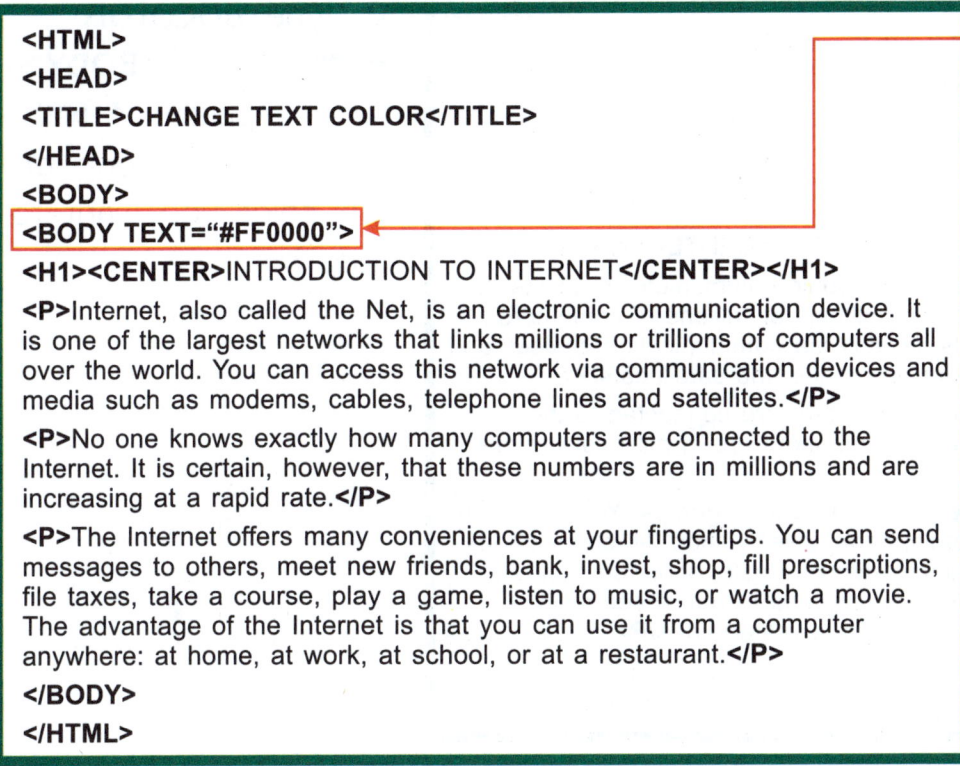

1. Type **TEXT ="*"** in the **<BODY>** tag, replacing * with the name or code of the color you want to use.

For example, if you want to change the text into red color, type: **<BODY TEXT = "FF0000">**

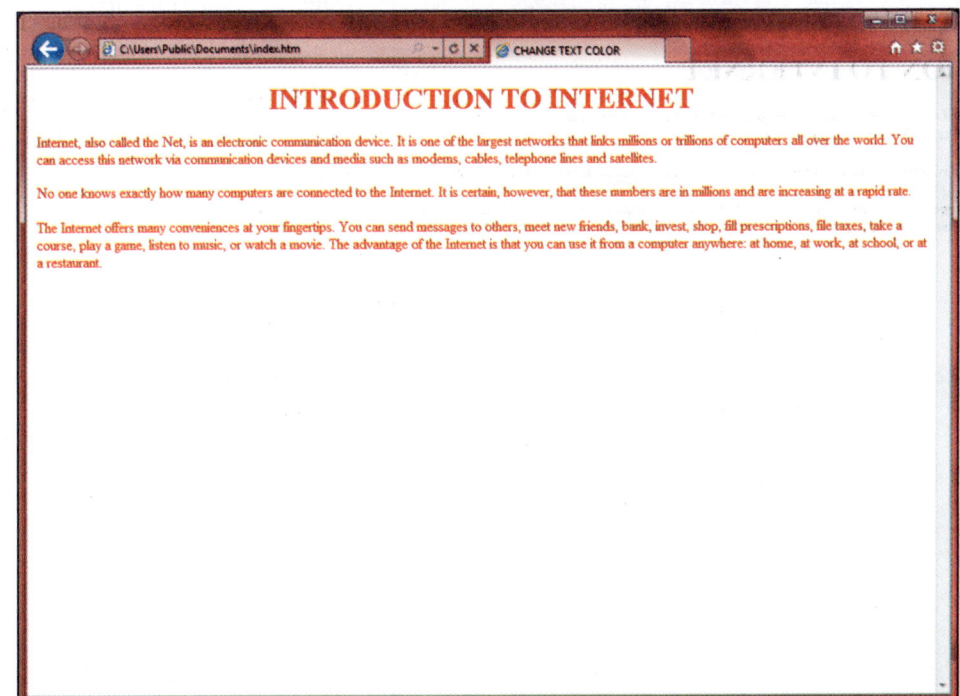

The web page with the font color you specified is displayed by the web browser.

There are 16 different colors which you can specify by particular names and choosing the font color of your text.

23

Drag and Drop Series

CHANGING THE BACKGROUND COLOR

By changing the background color, you can make your web page look more attractive and enhance the appearance of your text.

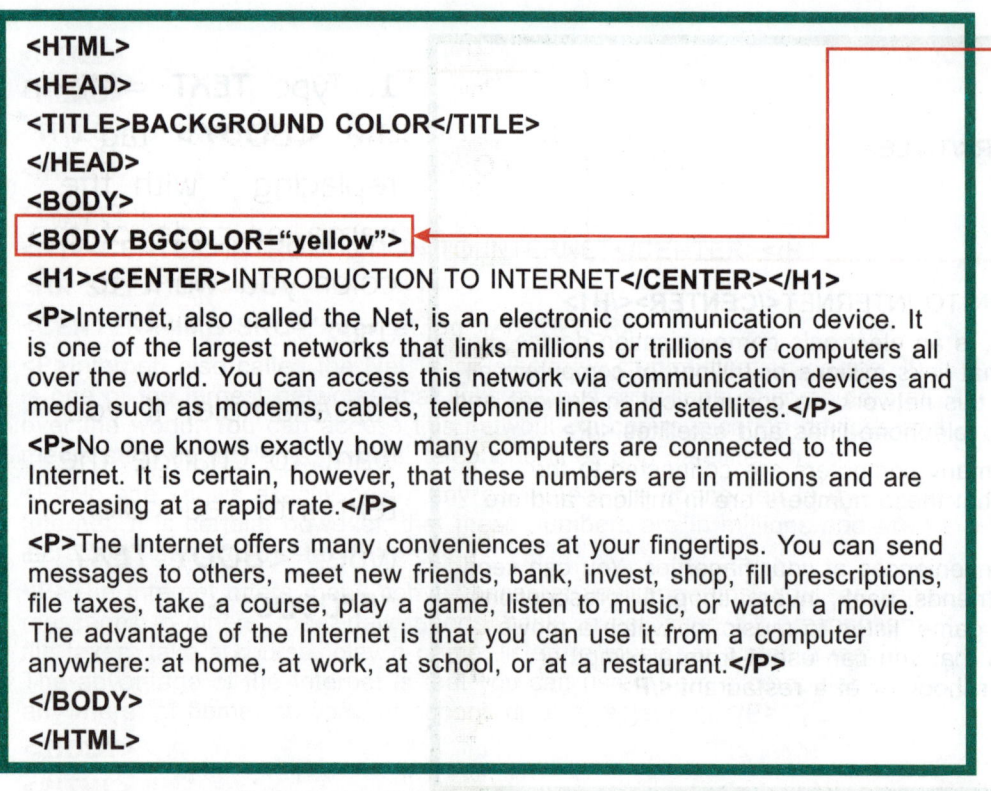

1. Type **BGCOLOR ="*"** in the **<BODY>** tag, replacing * with the name or code of the color you want to use.

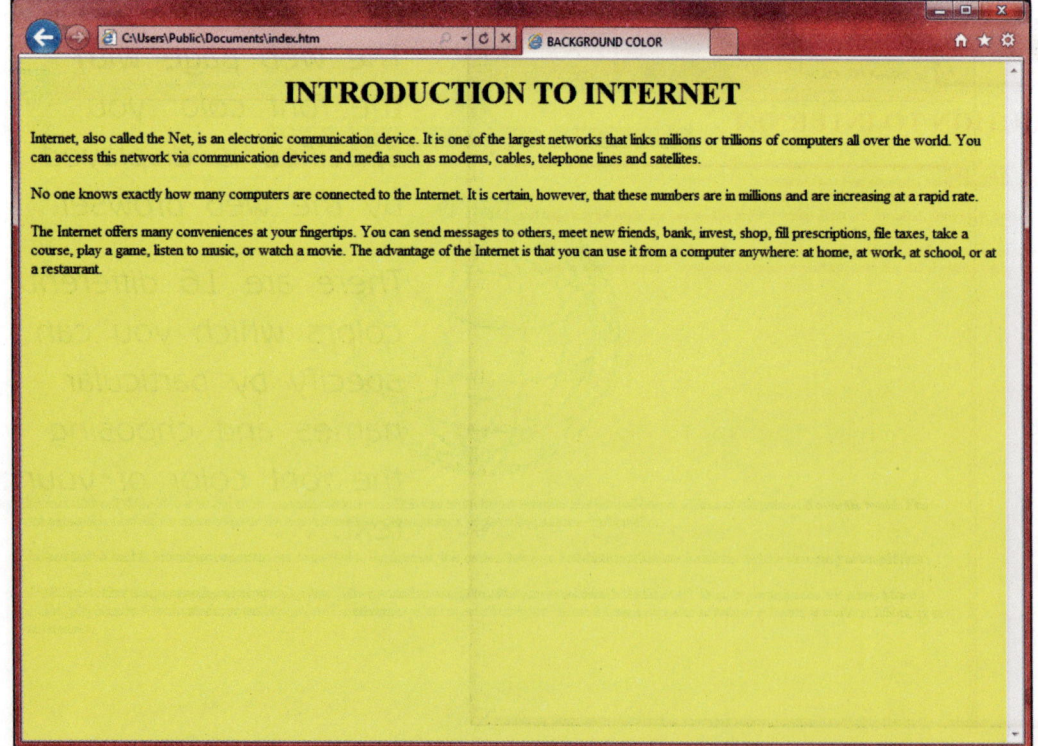

The web browser displays the web page with the specified background color.

There are 16 colors which you can specify by choosing the background color of your text.

HTML

COLOUR CODES

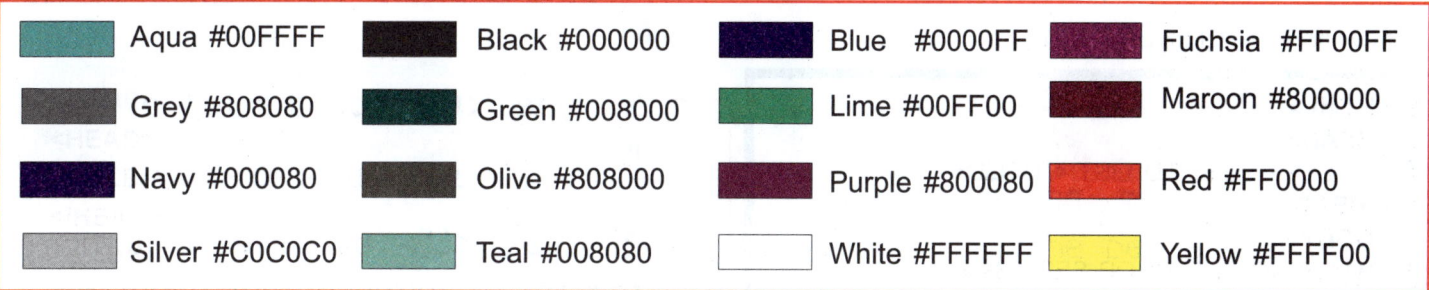

16 colours which you can specify by name

Name	Code
Black	#000000
Dark Blue	#0000CC
Medium Blue	#0000CD
Darkcyan	#008B8B
Deepskyblue	#00BFFF
Darkturquoise	#00CED1
Springgreen	#00FF7F
Lightseagreen	#20B2AA
Forestgreen	#228B22
Seagreen	#2E8B57
Darkslategrey	#2F4F4F
Limegreen	#32CD32
Royalblue	#4169E1
Steelblue	#4682B4
Darkslateblue	#483D8B
Indigo	#4B0082
Brown	#A52A2A

Name	Code
Darkolivegreen	#556B2F
Cadetblue	#5F9EA0
Cornflowerblue	#6495ED
Dimgrey	#696969
Lawngreen	#76FC00
Maroon	#800000
Purple	#800080
Lightskyblue	#87CEFA
Darkred	#8B0000
Darkmagenta	#8B008B
Saddlebrown	#8B4513
Palegreen	#98FB98
Yellowgreen	#9ACD32
Greenyellow	#ADFF2F
Powderblue	#B0E0E6
Firebrick	#B22222
Darkgoldenred	#B8860B

Name	Code
Rosybrown	#BC8F8F
Crimson	#DC143C
Plum	#DDA0DD
Violet	#EE82EE
Wheat	#F5DEB3
Whitesmoke	#F5F5F5
Mintcream	#F5FFFA
Salmon	#FA8072
Linen	#FAF0E6
Deeppink	#FF1493
Orangered	#FF4500
Tomato	#FF6347
Orange	#FFA500
Pink	#FFC0CB
Gold	#FFD700
Ivory	#FFFFF0

Drag and Drop Series

CREATING AN ORDERED LIST

You can create an ordered list for displaying the items in your text in a specified order. For example, set of instructions or a table of contents. Various styles can be followed in creating a list.

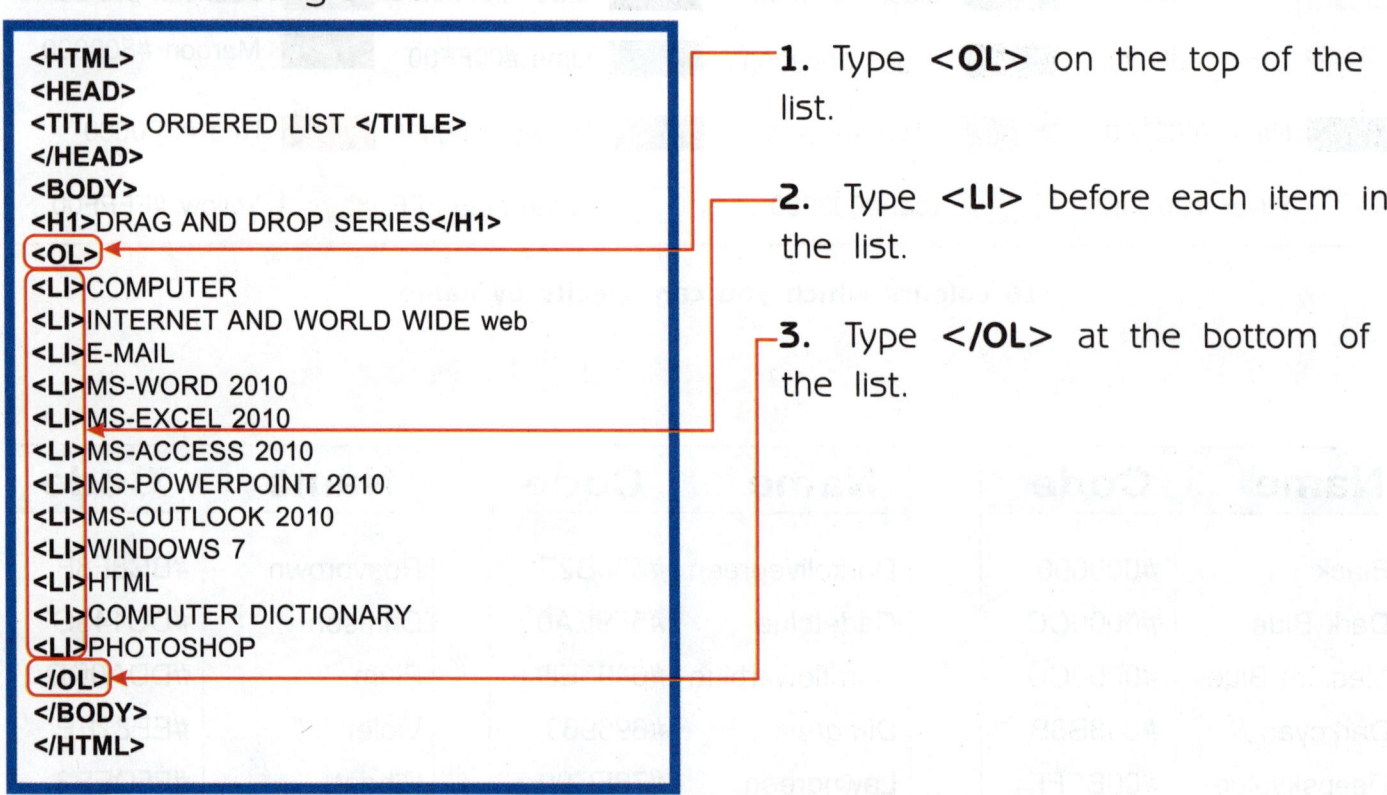

1. Type **<OL>** on the top of the list.

2. Type **<LI>** before each item in the list.

3. Type **</OL>** at the bottom of the list.

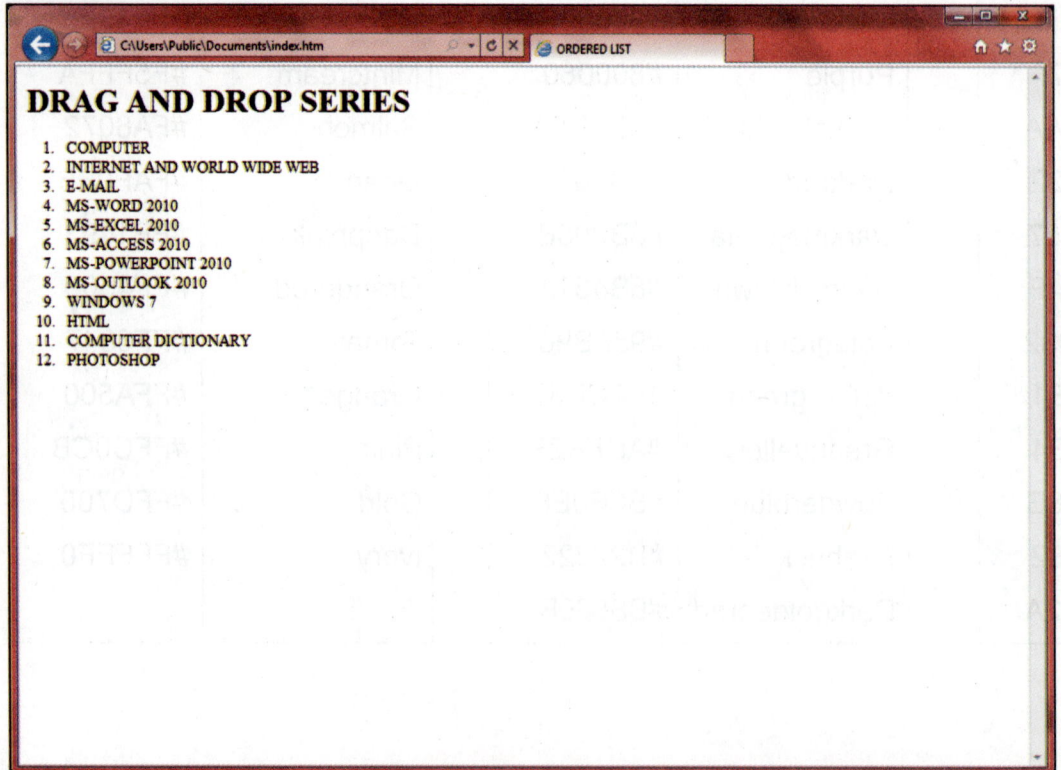

The ordered list is displayed by the web browser. A number appears before each item in the list.

CHANGING THE STYLE OF THE LIST

You can change the style of the number in an ordered list.

```
<HTML>
<HEAD>
<TITLE> ROMAN STYLE LIST </TITLE>
</HEAD>
<BODY>
<H1>DRAG AND DROP SERIES</H1>
<OL TYPE=i>
<LI>COMPUTER
<LI>INTERNET AND WORLD WIDE web
<LI>E-MAIL
<LI>MS-WORD 2010
<LI>MS-EXCEL 2010
<LI>MS-ACCESS 2010
<LI>MS-POWERPOINT 2010
<LI>MS-OUTLOOK 2010
<LI>WINDOWS 7
<LI>HTML
<LI>COMPUTER DICTIONARY
<LI>PHOTOSHOP
</OL>
</BODY>
</HTML>
```

1. In the **<OL>** tag, type **TYPE = ***, replacing ***** with the number style you want to use.

For example, if you wish to use Roman numbers in your ordered list, type **<OL TYPE = I>**.

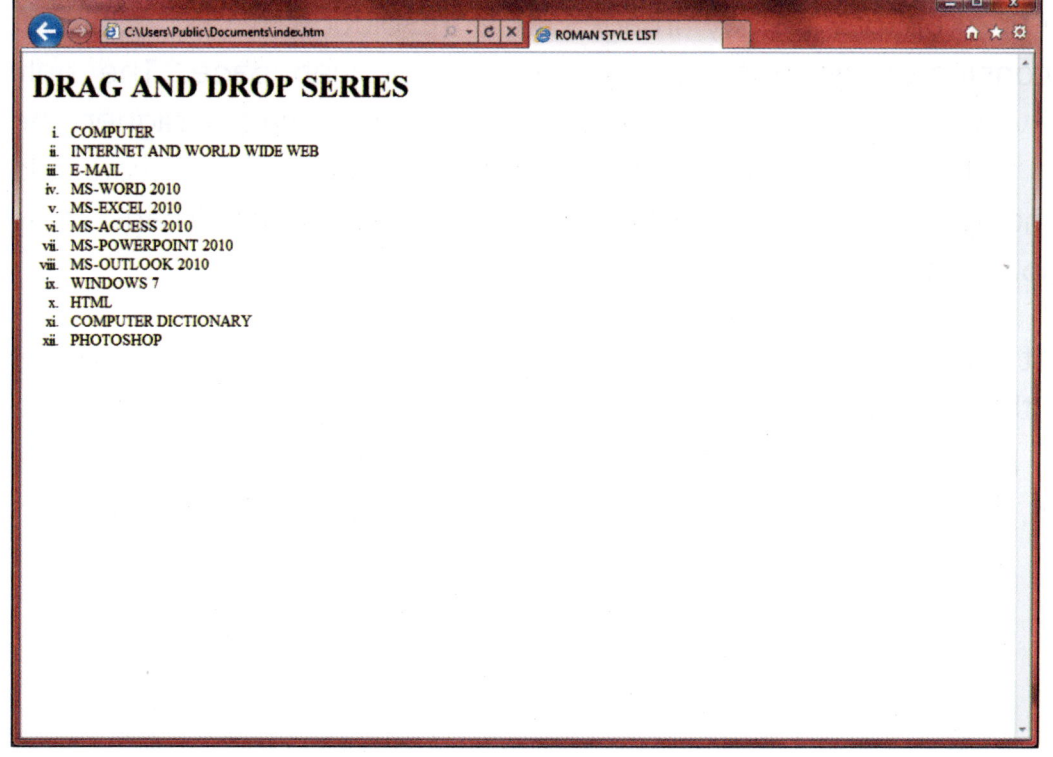

The ordered list with the Roman numbers is displayed by the web browser.

3 Adding images to a web page

IMAGES

An image plays a very important role in the web page. A web page can display drawings, paintings or computer-generated art. Companies can display their products on the web page so that people can view them and make an online purchase.

A concept which is difficult to explain in the text can be explained with the help of pictures on the web page. Readers can select the images and move backward or forward through the web pages. Most web sites offer you free images on your web page.

You can scan photographs, logos and drawings with the help of a scanner and then use the scanned images on your web page. Before using the image, you must make sure that these images are in a format that web browsers can display, such as **GIF** or **JPEG**. Higher resolution images are sharper and more detailed. Most computer monitors display images at a resolution of 72 dots per inch (dpi), which is considered good enough for use on a web page. The only drawback is that the viewer cannot get a paper copy of the image. Higher the resolution, the longer it takes to transfer to a computer. The images you add to your web page should be less than 620 pixels wide. A wider image may not fit on some computer screens.

If an image you want to add is stored in the same folder as the web page, you can specify just the name of the image (example: internet.jpg) in order to add it to your web page. If an image is stored in a sub-folder, you must specify the name of the sub-folder and the name of the image (example: images/internet.jpg).

IMG (IMAGE ELEMENT)

IMG stands for 'image'. It tells the browser where an image is located on the page. The image will pop up right where you write in the image tag. **SRC** stands for 'source'. This again is an attribute, a command inside a command. It tells the browser where to go to find the image. It's best for you to place the images you want to use in the same directory as the page. This way you can identify for the image by its name.

The IMG tag which specifies an image is displayed in HTML document. The IMG element has **SRC**, **ALIGN**, **BORDER**, **HEIGHT**, **WIDTH** and **ALT** as its attributes.

<IMG SRC="internet.jpg">

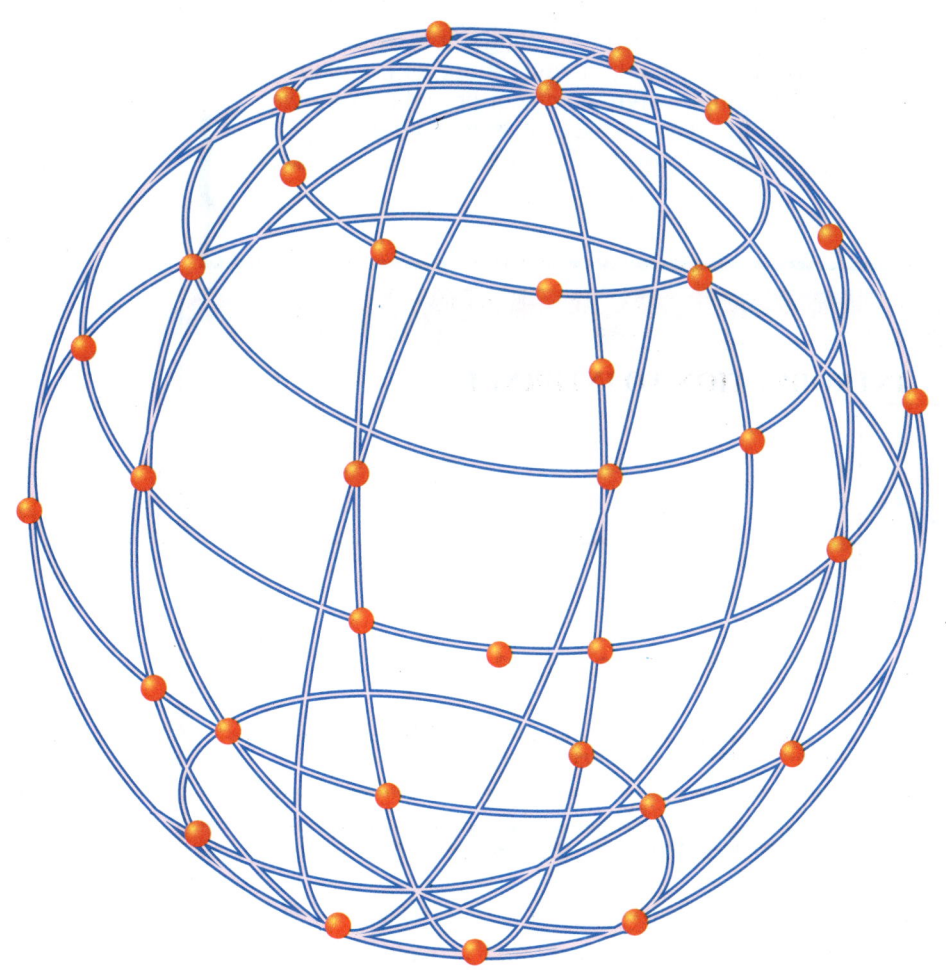

ADDING AN IMAGE

You can add an image to convey the purpose and enhance the looks of your web page. You should store all of your web pages and images in one folder in your computer.

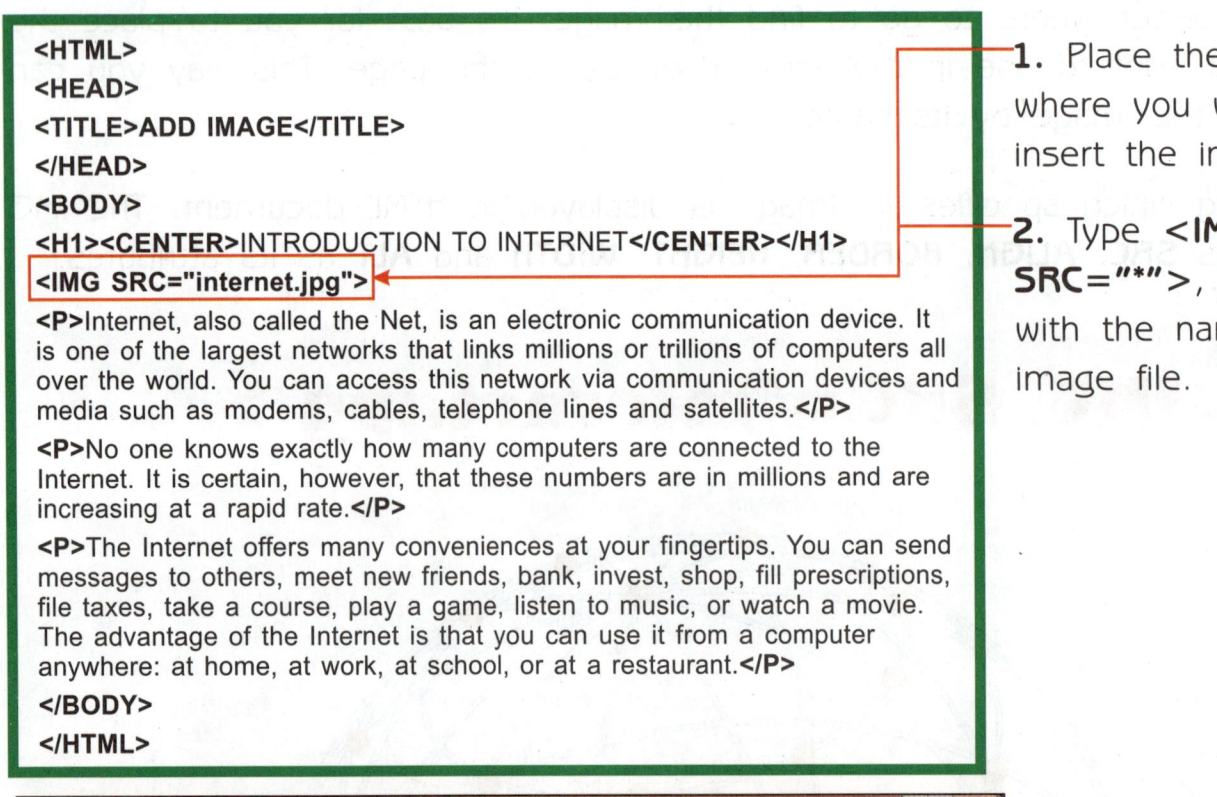

1. Place the cursor where you want to insert the image.

2. Type **<IMG SRC="*">**, replacing * with the name of the image file.

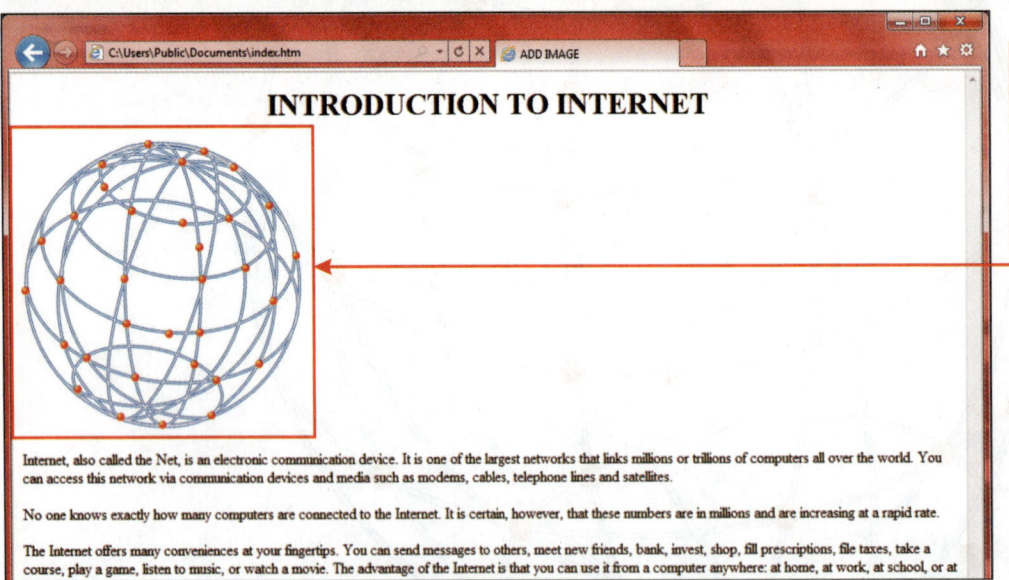

— The web browser displays the image on your web page.

While typing the name of the image file in step 2, make sure that this internet.jpg file exists in the folder in which your web page is stored. If not, then you have to specify the full path to the location of the image file.

CENTRE ALIGN AN IMAGE

Center align an image perform the following steps:

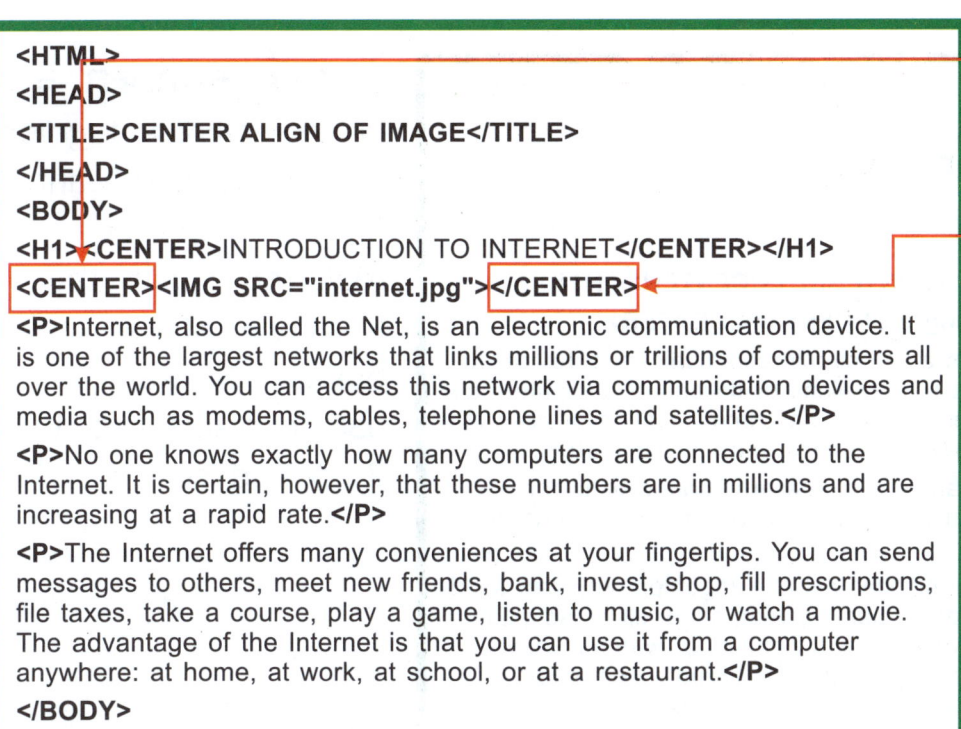

1. Type **<CENTER>** before the image you want to center.

2. Type **</CENTER>** after the image you want to center align.

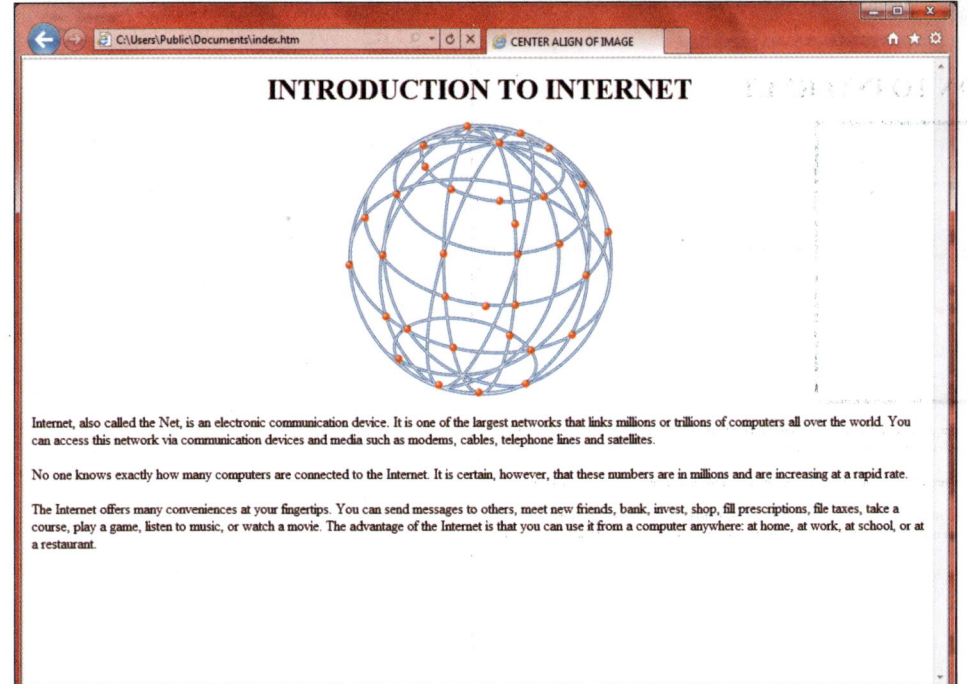

The image is displayed by the web browser with the specified alignment.

Drag and Drop Series

ADDING A BORDER TO AN IMAGE

You can create a frame around an image by specifying the width around the border of the image.

```
<HTML>
<HEAD>
<TITLE>ADD BORDER TO IMAGE</TITLE>
</HEAD>
<BODY>
<H1><CENTER>INTRODUCTION TO INTERNET</CENTER></H1>
<CENTER><IMG SRC="internet.jpg" BORDER=5></CENTER>
<P>Internet, also called the Net, is an electronic communication device. It is one of the largest networks that links millions or trillions of computers all over the world. You can access this network via communication devices and media such as modems, cables, telephone lines and satellites.</P>
<P>No one knows exactly how many computers are connected to the Internet. It is certain, however, that these numbers are in millions and are increasing at a rapid rate.</P>
<P>The Internet offers many conveniences at your fingertips. You can send messages to others, meet new friends, bank, invest, shop, fill prescriptions, file taxes, take a course, play a game, listen to music, or watch a movie. The advantage of the Internet is that you can use it from a computer anywhere: at home, at work, at school, or at a restaurant.</P>
</BODY>
</HTML>
```

1. Type, **BORDER = *** in the **<IMG>** tag for the image you want to give a border, replacing ***** with the thickness of the border you want to use in pixels like 1, 2, 3 and so on.

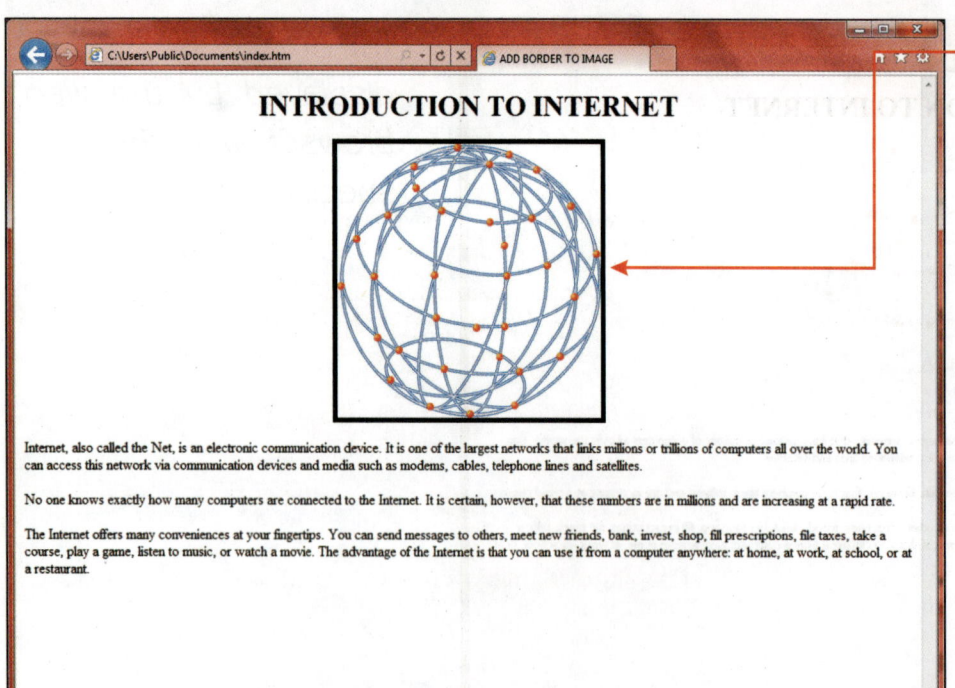

The web browser displays the image with a border around it on your web page.

To remove an existing border, specify the width with number 0. For example, <IMG SRC = "internet.jpg" BORDER = 0>

WRAPPING TEXT AROUND THE IMAGE

You can wrap text around an image to render a more professional look to the web page.

```
<HTML>
<HEAD>
<TITLE>WRAP TEXT</TITLE>
</HEAD>
<BODY>
<H1><CENTER>INTRODUCTION TO INTERNET</CENTER></H1>
<IMG SRC="internet.jpg" ALIGN=left>
<P>Internet, also called the Net, is an electronic communication device. It is one of the largest networks that links millions or trillions of computers all over the world. You can access this network via communication devices and media such as modems, cables, telephone lines and satellites.</P>
<P>No one knows exactly how many computers are connected to the Internet. It is certain, however, that these numbers are in millions and are increasing at a rapid rate.</P>
<P>The Internet offers many conveniences at your fingertips. You can send messages to others, meet new friends, bank, invest, shop, fill prescriptions, file taxes, take a course, play a game, listen to music, or watch a movie. The advantage of the Internet is that you can use it from a computer anywhere: at home, at work, at school, or at a restaurant.</P>
</BODY>
</HTML>
```

1. Type **ALIGN = left** in the **<IMG>** tag of the image to wrap text around the right side of an image.

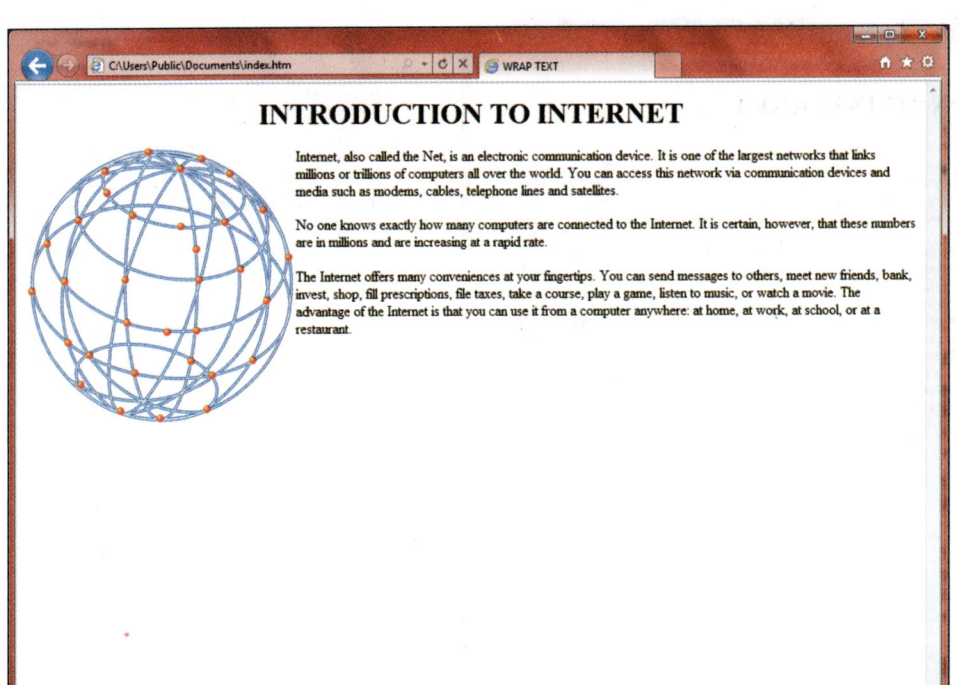

The text wrapped around the image appears in the web browser.

Type ALIGN = right in the <IMG> tag of the image to wrap text around the left side of the image.

Drag and Drop Series

WRAPPING THE TEXT BETWEEN TWO IMAGES

You can wrap text between two images to change the layout of your web page.

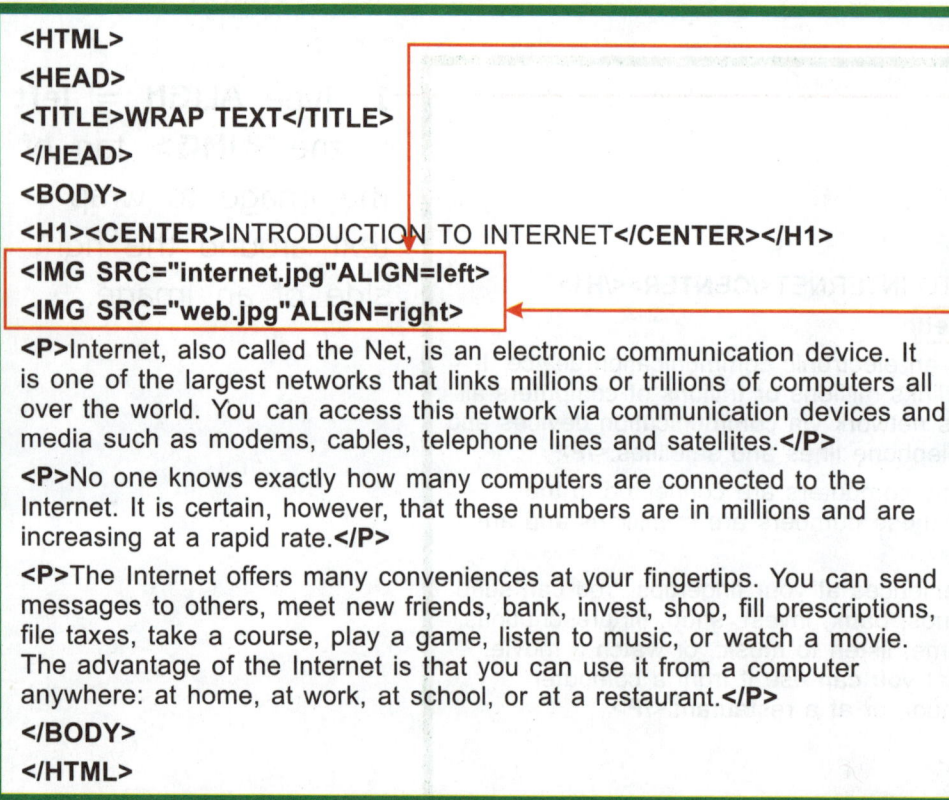

1. In the **<IMG>** tag for the image you want to appear on the left side of text, type **ALIGN=left**.

2. In the **<IMG>** tag for the image you want to appear on the right side of text, type **ALIGN=right**.

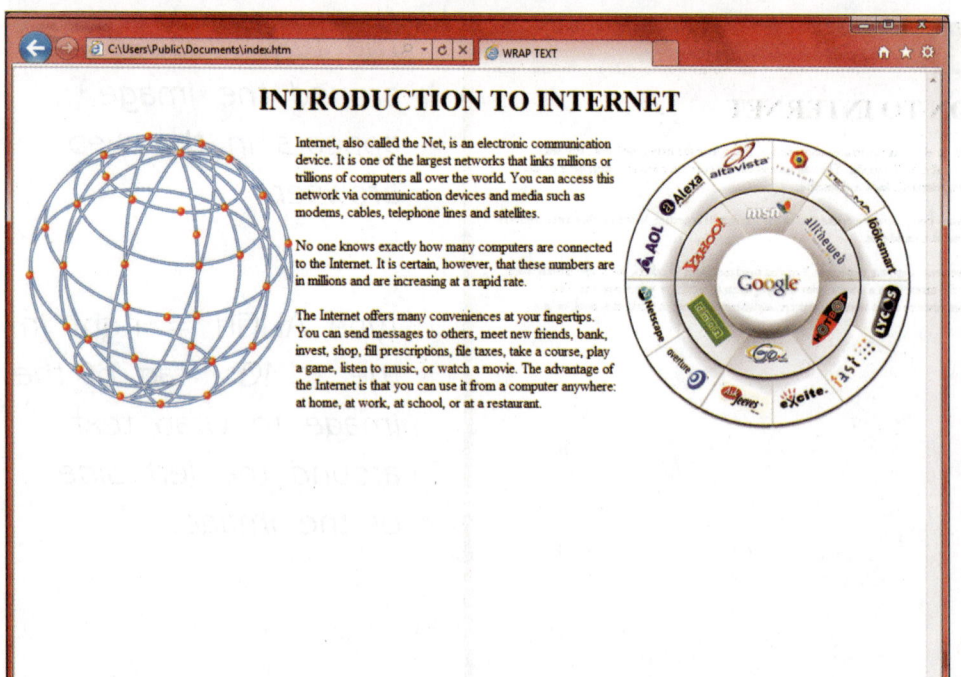

The text wrapped around the two images appears in the web browser.

ADDING SPACE AROUND THE IMAGE

You can add some gap between an image and the surrounding text. It makes the text easier to read.

```
<HTML>
<HEAD>
<TITLE>ADD SPACE BETWEEN IMAGE</TITLE>
</HEAD>
<BODY>
<H1><CENTER>INTRODUCTION TO INTERNET</CENTER></H1>
<IMG SRC="internet.jpg"ALIGN=left HSPACE=40>
<P>Internet, also called the Net, is an electronic communication device. It is one of the largest networks that links millions or trillions of computers all over the world. You can access this network via communication devices and media such as modems, cables, telephone lines and satellites.</P>
<P>No one knows exactly how many computers are connected to the Internet. It is certain, however, that these numbers are in millions and are increasing at a rapid rate.</P>
<P>The Internet offers many conveniences at your fingertips. You can send messages to others, meet new friends, bank, invest, shop, fill prescriptions, file taxes, take a course, play a game, listen to music, or watch a movie. The advantage of the Internet is that you can use it from a computer anywhere: at home, at work, at school, or at a restaurant.</P>
</BODY>
</HTML>
```

1. Type **HSPACE =*** in the **<IMG>** tag for the image you want to add space around, replacing * with the amount of space you want to add to both the left and right sides of the image in pixels.

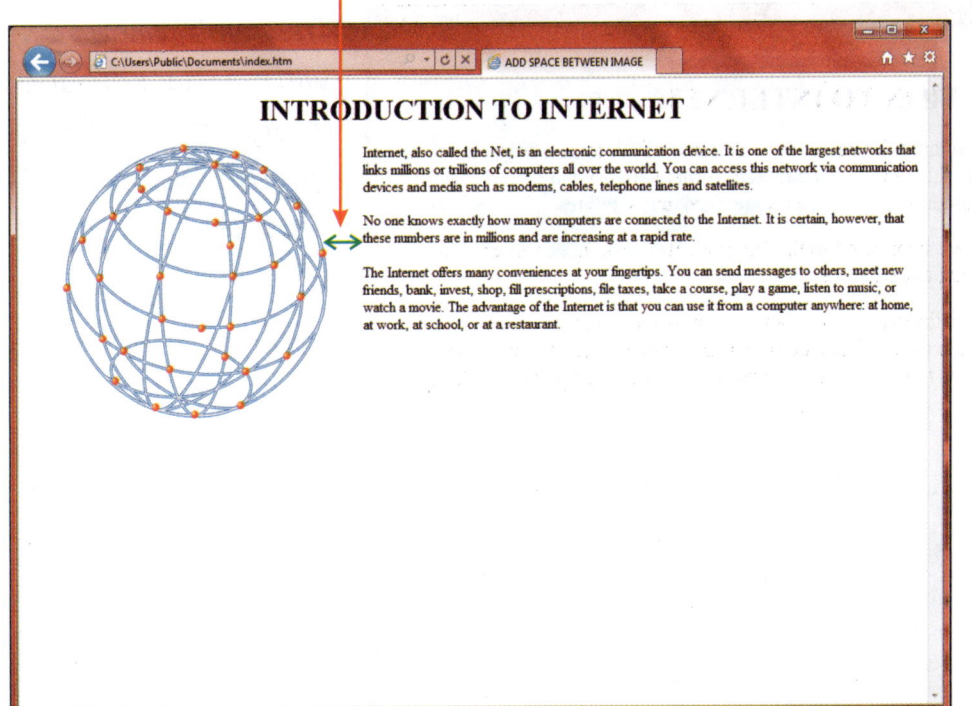

― The image with the specified margin around it appears in the web browser.

Drag and Drop Series

ADDING A BACKGROUND IMAGE

You can add a background image to improve the layout of the entire page. However, adding these background images increases the amount of time for a web page to appear on screen.

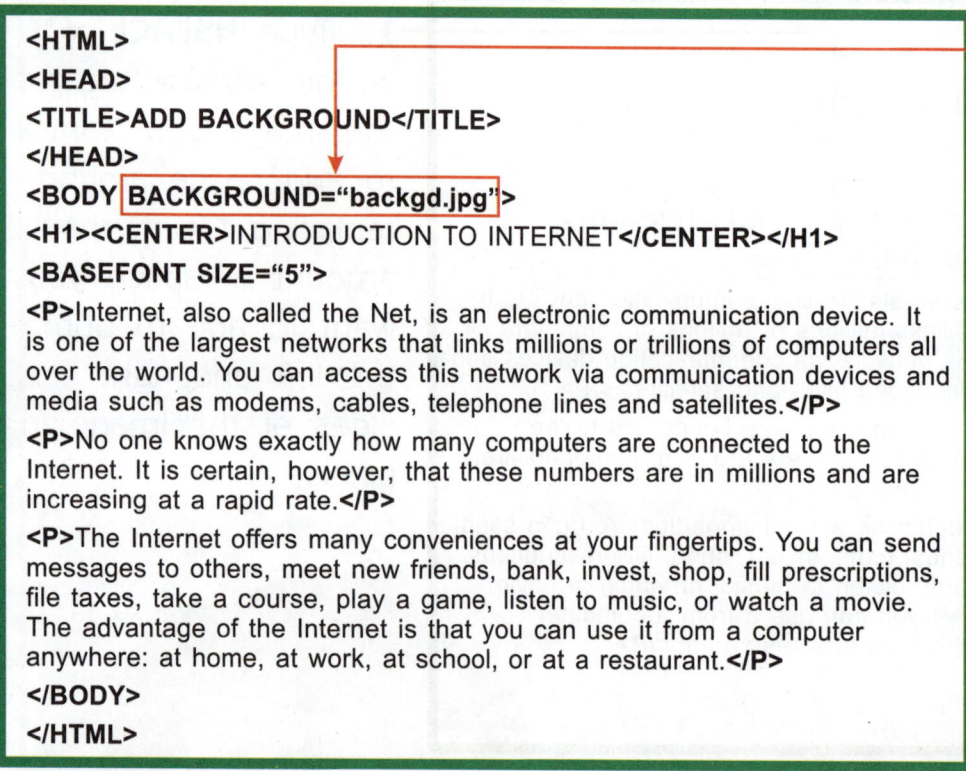

```
<HTML>
<HEAD>
<TITLE>ADD BACKGROUND</TITLE>
</HEAD>
<BODY BACKGROUND="backgd.jpg">
<H1><CENTER>INTRODUCTION TO INTERNET</CENTER></H1>
<BASEFONT SIZE="5">
<P>Internet, also called the Net, is an electronic communication device. It is one of the largest networks that links millions or trillions of computers all over the world. You can access this network via communication devices and media such as modems, cables, telephone lines and satellites.</P>
<P>No one knows exactly how many computers are connected to the Internet. It is certain, however, that these numbers are in millions and are increasing at a rapid rate.</P>
<P>The Internet offers many conveniences at your fingertips. You can send messages to others, meet new friends, bank, invest, shop, fill prescriptions, file taxes, take a course, play a game, listen to music, or watch a movie. The advantage of the Internet is that you can use it from a computer anywhere: at home, at work, at school, or at a restaurant.</P>
</BODY>
</HTML>
```

1. Type **BACKGROUND = "*"** in the **<BODY>** tag, replacing * with the location and name of the background file on your computer.

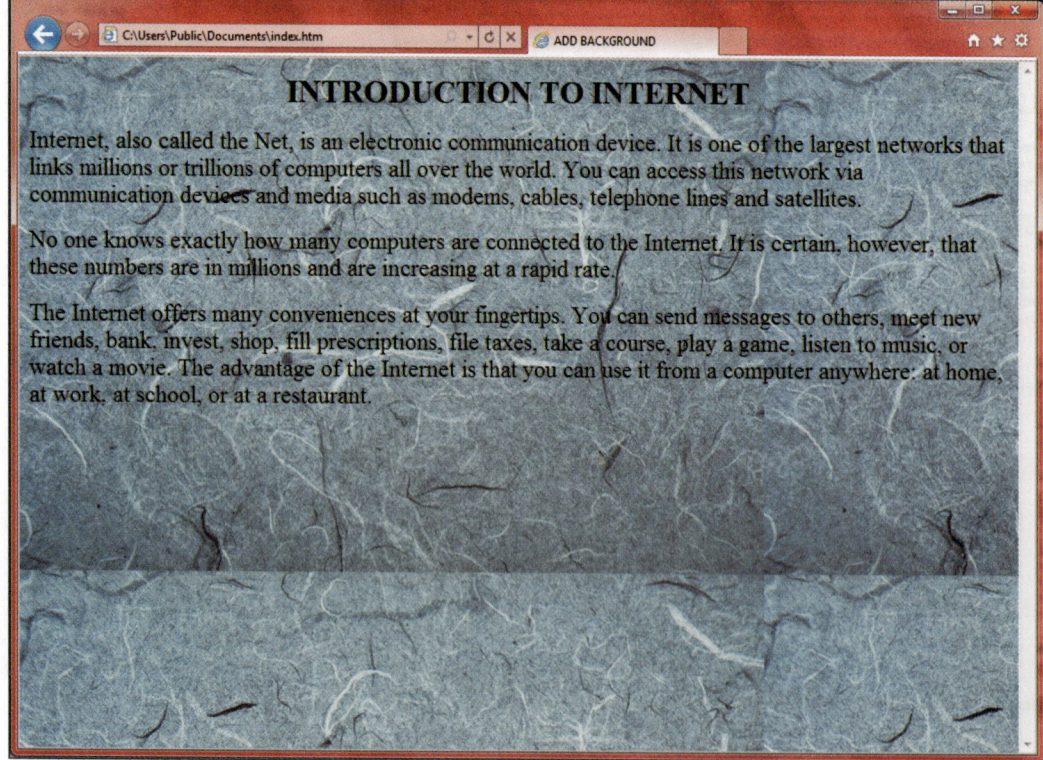

The web page with a background image is displayed by the web browser.

4 Horizontal rule

ADDING A HORIZONTAL RULE

You can add a horizontal rule or line to separate different sections of your web page.

```
<HTML>
<HEAD>
<TITLE>HORIZONTAL RULE</TITLE>
</HEAD>
<BODY>
<H1><CENTER>INTRODUCTION TO INTERNET</CENTER></H1>
<HR>
<CENTER><IMG SRC="internet.jpg"></CENTER>
<P>Internet, also called the Net, is an electronic communication device. It is one of the largest networks that links millions or trillions of computers all over the world. You can access this network via communication devices and media such as modems, cables, telephone lines and satellites.</P>
<P>No one knows exactly how many computers are connected to the Internet. It is certain, however, that these numbers are in millions and are increasing at a rapid rate.</P>
<P>The Internet offers many conveniences at your fingertips. You can send messages to others, meet new friends, bank, invest, shop, fill prescriptions, file taxes, take a course, play a game, listen to music, or watch a movie. The advantage of the Internet is that you can use it from a computer anywhere: at home, at work, at school, or at a restaurant.</P>
</BODY></HTML>
```

1. Type **<HR>** where you want to insert a horizontal rule on your web page.

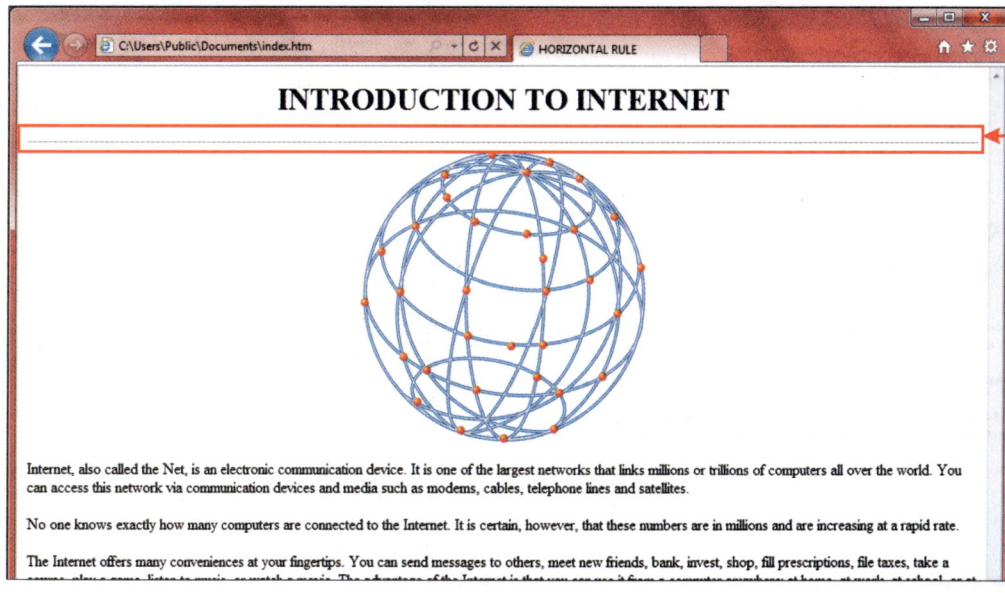

The horizontal rule on your web page is displayed by the web browser.

Drag and Drop Series

CHANGING THE THICKNESS OF HORIZONTAL RULE

You can change the thickness of horizontal rule in the web page for better viewing.

```
<HTML>
<HEAD>
<TITLE>THICKNESS OF HORIZONTAL RULE</TITLE>
</HEAD>
<BODY>
<H1><CENTER>INTRODUCTION TO INTERNET</CENTER></H1>
<HR SIZE=10>
<CENTER><IMG SRC="internet.jpg"></CENTER>
<P>Internet, also called the Net, is an electronic communication device. It is one of the largest networks that links millions or trillions of computers all over the world. You can access this network via communication devices and media such as modems, cables, telephone lines and satellites.</P>
<P>No one knows exactly how many computers are connected to the Internet. It is certain, however, that these numbers are in millions and are increasing at a rapid rate.</P>
<P>The Internet offers many conveniences at your fingertips. You can send messages to others, meet new friends, bank, invest, shop, fill prescriptions, file taxes, take a course, play a game, listen to music, or watch a movie. The advantage of the Internet is that you can use it from a computer anywhere: at home, at work, at school, or at a restaurant.</P>
</BODY>
</HTML>
```

1. Type **SIZE = "*"** in the **<HR>** tag, replacing ***** with the thickness you want to use for the horizontal rule.

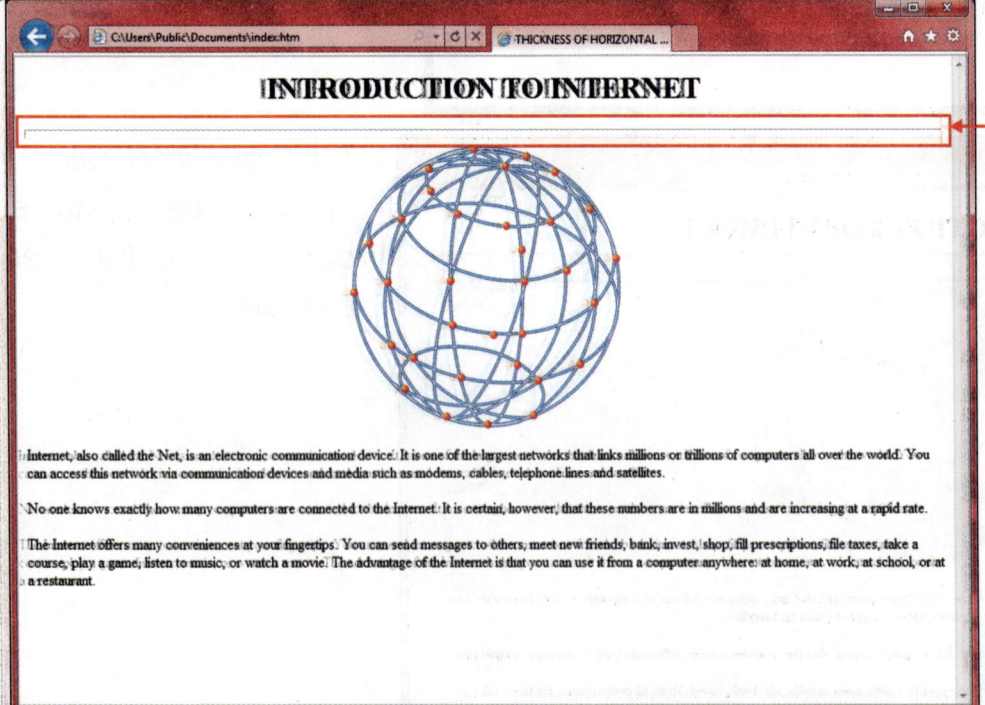

The horizontal rule with the thickness you specified appears in the web browser.

HTML

CHANGING THE WIDTH OF THE HORIZONTAL RULE

You can change the width of a horizontal rule, if you do not want the rule to extend across the entire web page.

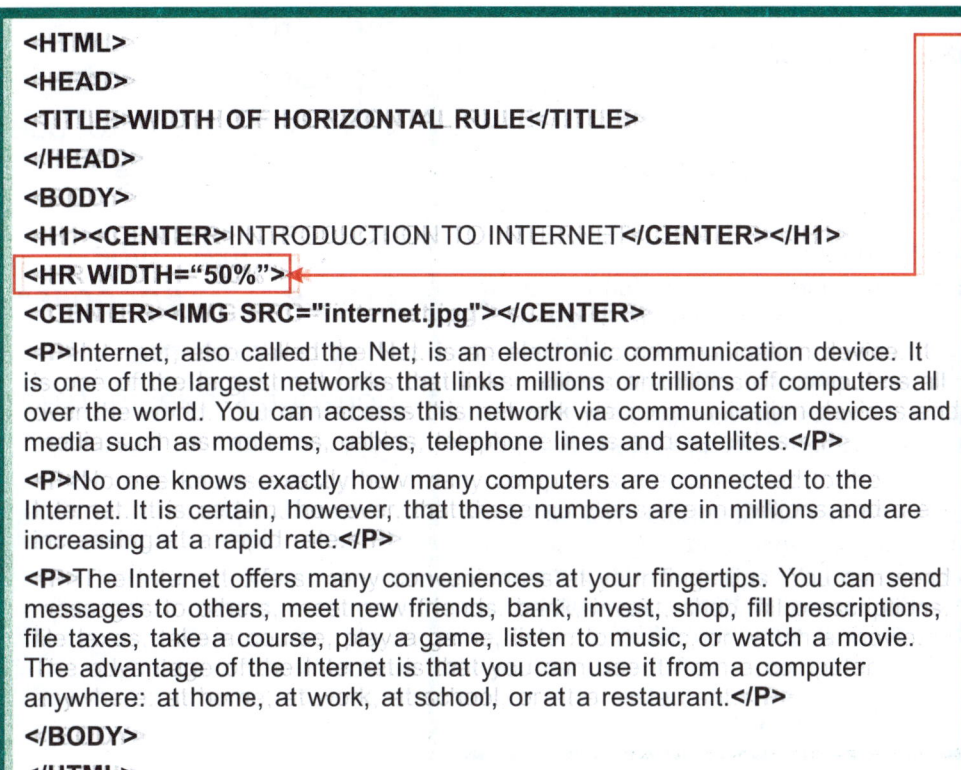

1. Type **WIDTH = "*%"** in the **<HR>** tag, replacing * with the percentage of the horizontal rule to extend across the web page.

For example, type 50% if you wish to extend the horizontal rule to halfway across the web page.

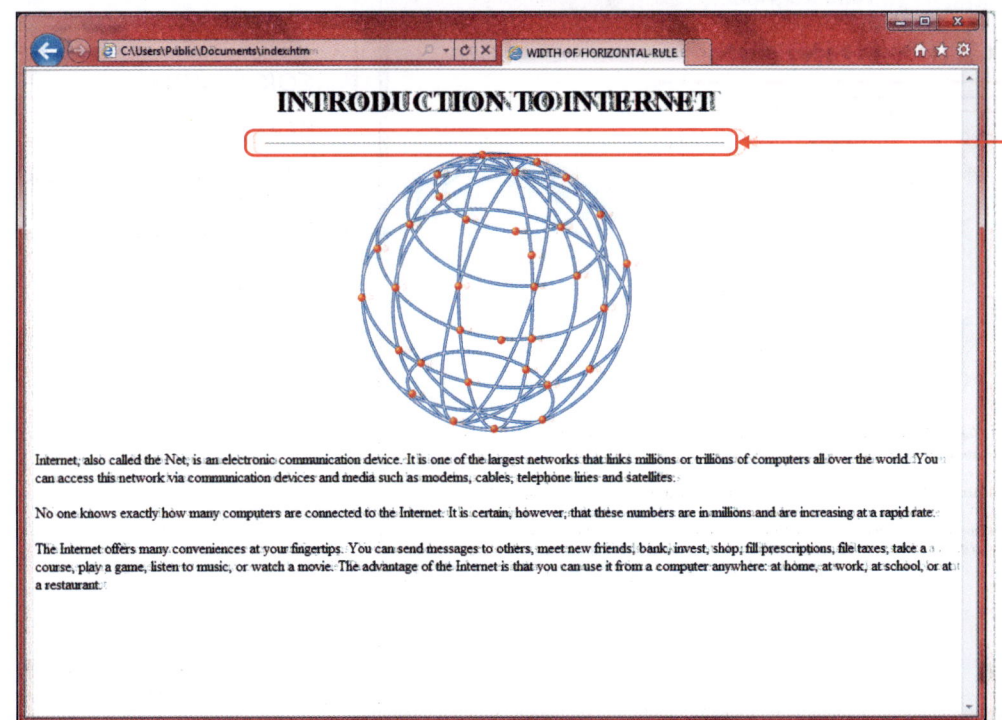

The horizontal rule with the new width on your web page is shown by the web browser.

Drag and Drop Series

CHANGING THE COLOR OF THE HORIZONTAL RULE

You can change the color of the horizontal rule in your web page.

```
<HTML>
<HEAD>
<TITLE>CHANGE COLOR OF HORIZONTAL RULE</TITLE>
</HEAD>
<BODY>
<H1><CENTER>INTRODUCTION TO INTERNET</CENTER></H1>
<HR WIDTH="50%" COLOR= "#0000FF">
<CENTER><IMG SRC="internet.jpg"></CENTER>
<P>Internet, also called the Net, is an electronic communication device. It is one of the largest networks that links millions or trillions of computers all over the world. You can access this network via communication devices and media such as modems, cables, telephone lines and satellites.</P>
<P>No one knows exactly how many computers are connected to the Internet. It is certain, however, that these numbers are in millions and are increasing at a rapid rate.</P>
<P>The Internet offers many conveniences at your fingertips. You can send messages to others, meet new friends, bank, invest, shop, fill prescriptions, file taxes, take a course, play a game, listen to music, or watch a movie. The advantage of the Internet is that you can use it from a computer anywhere: at home, at work, at school, or at a restaurant.</P>
</BODY>
</HTML>
```

1. Type **COLOR="*"** in the **<HR>** tag, replacing ***** With the color you want to use in horizontal rule.

For example, type **COLOR = "#0000FF"** *if you want the horizontal rule in blue color.*

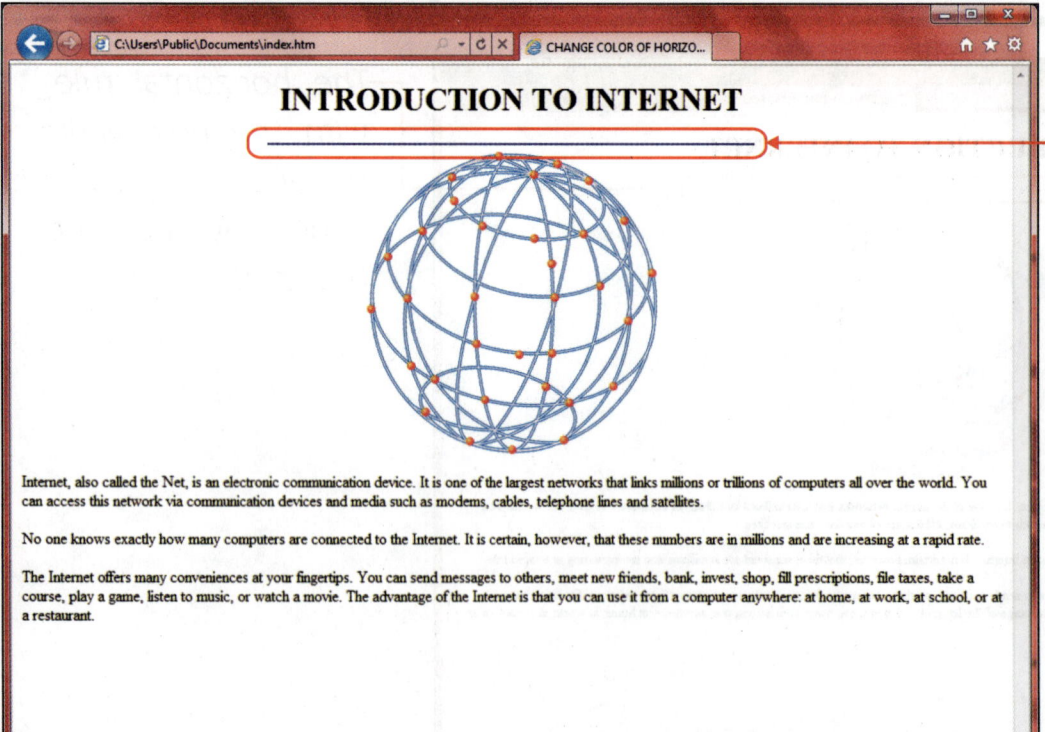

The horizontal rule with the color you specified is displayed by the web browser.

40